Skelligs Sunset

Skelligs Sunset
MICHAEL KIRBY

The Lilliput Press, Dublin
2006

First published 2006 by
The Lilliput Press
62–63 Sitric Road, Arbour Hill
Dublin 7, Ireland
www.lilliputpress.ie

ISBN 1 84351 083 9

A CIP record for this title is available
from The British Library.

10 9 8 7 6 5 4 3 2 1

Set in 11.5 pt on 14.2 pt Sabon
Printed in England by MPG Books, Bodmin, Cornwall

CONTENTS

PREFACE

When Michael Kirby died in April 2005 he left a considerable body of writing in the English language, some of which he had been working on up to the very last months of his life. It includes recollections of life in the Iveragh region of County Kerry during his childhood; essays; poems; folklore and fiction. The work was written with a view to publication as a companion volume to his earlier books, *Skelligs Calling* and *Skelligside*. Michael Kirby had even prepared an introduction and chosen a title: it was to be, and is, *Skelligs Sunset*. The title acknowledges his mortality and recognizes that this was to be his last book.

Most of its contents were written in the five years before his death; some pieces, such as 'Humpty-Dumpty', 'My Garden', 'Schooldays: Tug of War in the Classroom' and his 'Introduction', as late as 2004. Although he was by then in his late nineties and physically weakened, there was no dulling of his intellect, no falter in his recall of the past. His voice remained clear and distinctive to the end.

However, without his guiding presence, there are some challenges for the editor. In line with his practice and principles, it is likely that he would have reworked at least some of the pieces included here. In the preface to his first book in English, *Skelligside*, he recalls that the schoolmaster who taught him in the national school in the second decade of the twentieth century 'was a stickler for accuracy, and when English was in session he would growl and wield his hazel wand, shouting "Watch your grammar!" ' Michael learned the lesson well and displayed great respect for the formality of the written word. His style, therefore, is distinctive and complex: it combines the charm and immediacy of the traditional *seanchaí* with the self-conscious formality of a written testament.

His family attests to the meticulous care he took in preparing for publication the contents of *Skelligs Calling* and *Skelligside,* and the manuscript evidence bears this out. Despite the demands that longhand makes, his habit was to redraft and reshape repeatedly. His script is distinctive: he employs an elegant cursive style. Each letter is carefully formed, and only his last manuscripts betray a slight tremor. Punctuation, however, commands less attention. Some poems, for example, have few, if any, punctuation marks.

Here, then, are pieces at varying stages of readiness for publication. They were transcribed in the first instance by Michael's son-in-law, Pat Coffey. In many cases all that was required of the editor was to standardize punctuation and spelling and correct the occasional grammatical or syntactical infelicity: many pieces bear the imprint of Michael Kirby's own critical reworking. However, some, in particular the stories, required more attention. Some digressions from the plot of the story 'Jerry No Name' were excised, as was some extraneous detail. Less substantial were the changes made to 'The Courting of Moll Molloy'. Some titles were modified. However, the chief editorial principle employed was restraint. The distinctiveness of the voice and the leisurely narrative approach were respected.

Furthermore, it seems that the tales told here are worthy of inclusion for reasons other than their narrative economy: Anne Coffey confirms that many were based on real events. Secondly, they derive from a tradition tolerant of a narrative approach that takes a scenic route before arriving at its destination.

The organizing principle adopted was that of a miscellany. The works are not presented either in the sequence in which they were written or according to genre (poetry, story and so on). Rather, they are broadly attuned to the rhythms of Michael Kirby's life. Thus, autobiographical material on childhood is placed near the beginning, together with memories of customs and old ways. Events, tales and information that might reasonably have come his way during adulthood, or that relate to the life of a young man – love, marriage and fishing, for example – come next. Interspersed throughout are poems whose content loosely relates to the lengthier prose compositions. Because Michael Kirby sometimes translated and refashioned work already published – from Irish to English and vice versa – the text of two Irish poems, 'Miangas' from *Íochtar Trá* and 'Coinne' from *Barra Taoide*, are included alongside free translations, 'Yearning' and 'Our First Forbidden Tryst'. The English version of 'Miangas' is published for the first time. ('Coinne' also appears, translated by the author, in *Skelligside*.)

The pieces placed last show Michael, now *'fé scáth na lice'* ('under the shadow of the gravestone'), to use his own phrase, but at peace with this world and ready for the imminent call to the next. The penultimate essay, 'A Painting is Born', ostensibly recounts Michael's interest in painting, developed only after he reached seventy years of age. However, it also acts as an *apologia pro vita sua*, a defence of his life, and a statement of its value. Painting may be read in this case as a metaphor for the effort, the care, the shaping that can make sense of a life, almost to the moment when the last breath is drawn.

This collection of Michael Kirby's last works is enriched by the addition of a foreword written by noted folklorist and scholar Dáithí Ó hÓgáin, who had the privilege of knowing Michael Kirby personally. He offers insights into Michael's humanity and dynamic presence, he evaluates his achievement, the literary and folk contexts that illuminate his work, and the breadth of his reading and knowledge. His essay will evoke the man and the place to those who come to Kirby and the Skelligs for the first time; and it will affectionately recall him to his friends.

I am greatly indebted to Anne Coffey and Pat Coffey for their assistance while editing this collection. In addition to being diligent proofreaders, they offered unique insight and invaluable guidance in interpreting Michael Kirby's approach to his writing. Maureen Granfield Hufnagle, Michael's grand-niece from Medfield, Massachusetts, and Timothy Kirby Forde, Michael's grandson, also assisted with proofreading.

Go dtuga Dia suaimhneas síoraí d'anam dílis Mhichíl.

Mary Shine Thompson, Editor

FOREWORD

During the Easter holidays in 1971 I was in County Kerry, trying to find out all I could about poets and poetry in the whole area west of Killarney as far as the sea. This had been for centuries one of the most learned parts of Ireland, the stamping ground in the nineteenth century of Seán Crón and Séamas Crón Ó Súilleabháin, Siobhán Ní Iarlaithe, Diarmaid Ó Gealbháin, Seán Ó Siochrú, Diarmaid Ó Fáilbhe, Micheál Ó Meára, Seán Vácúir Ó Súilleabháin and many more. I spent several days in the shadow of the Macgillicuddy Reeks searching for lingering memories of these old poets and legendary accounts of their travails, their courage, and their magical speech; a whole tradition that had been receding since the time of the Great Famine. Folklore collectors under the direction of Professor Séamus Ó Duilearga – and particularly the brilliant folklorist of Iveragh, Tadhg Ó Murchú – had, a generation or two earlier, assembled a large body of such lore, as well as many substantial oral poems that would otherwise have been lost forever.

I wanted to find out if anything of any relevance had been left uncollected, and in my work I got most generous help from several people in that whole area – Killarney, Glencar, Glenbeigh, Killorglin and Beaufort – that helped to fill in the history and local context. Everything was fitting into shape, but there was one major remaining problem – there were some words and expressions found in no dictionary but put to fine creative use by these old poets of a century and more before, and I needed somebody with special knowledge of the specific Irish dialect of south-west Kerry to help me with this. So I went farther west, and I found my man; a man who in addition to being a native speaker of Irish since his birth was also himself an accomplished poet. That man was Michael Kirby.

The first thing I noticed about this man of Ballinskelligs was that he had the bearing of a chieftain. A very tall man, already advancing in years, but with unusually handsome looks, a slow and deliberate voice and a fine aesthetic sense. Most striking of all, however, was his quiet manner, born of a natural courtesy and of the mind of a philosopher. Michael was already a painter, a poet, and a deep thinker, but – looking back now on the generation and more that has passed since then – I, in common with many others, continue to be amazed by what he accomplished from that time onwards. It was as if a whole lifetime of observation, of thought, of investigation, of speculation and of computation had welled up within him and had begun to flow as a mighty river of creative energy. The hue of that river had indeed been touched, and repeatedly so, by the beautiful surroundings in which he grew up and by the love and companionship of his wife and family and friends, and its surges had been carried along by the tremendous vitality of the old language in which he was an expert. But, whatever its nature or its sources, that great river of creativity broke out when he was already an elderly man and, for the next twenty years and more, he produced book after book in both languages and covering a wide variety of styles and themes. I know of nobody else who began writing so late in life (he undertook it in a serious way only when he was in his late seventies), or who finished writing so late in life either: in the months before he died, almost in his hundredth year, no longer physically able to write, he continued to dictate his thoughts. In this regard Michael must forever stand as a unique figure in the literature of our country.

Michael Kirby (or Mícheál Ua Ciarmhaic, as he was better known) was born in Ballinskelligs in 1906, the youngest of a family of seven. His four brothers and two sisters all emigrated to the USA and settled there. He himself spent a short period on the other side of the Atlantic also. He married a local girl, Peggy O'Sullivan (Peig Ní Shúilleabháin), in 1943. They had six children, Anne, John (who died of meningitis at the age of two), Martina, Declan, Margaret and Tim. Always well known and held in affection and respect locally, he became known nationally through his writings. He died on 6 April 2005 and is buried in the new cemetery in Kinnard, half a mile from his home.

He was a great conversationalist, possessing an extraordinarily liberal mind for a man of his generation, engaging brilliantly with young and old on a wide variety of subjects, subjects to the significance of which he always added an extra dimension of his own. His wisdom was clear to all who heard him comment on topics as diverse as artistic theory, Irish history and folklore, world politics, fishing and farming, economics and community development. He loved to debate, but always in a spirit of inclusiveness, and rancour was never known to enter into his speech or mentality. He often described himself as a student of the world, and he was this in the fullest and widest sense. It has often been remarked that, in addition to its wonderful colour of expression, to survive and strengthen the Irish language needs to spread its wings wider and cover an ever-expanding scope of interest in the contemporary world. Michael showed the way in this – his interests being all-embracing and yet rooted in the lilting rhythm that, as a celebrated scholar once remarked, is everywhere the sign of the true Irish speaker.

He loved to tease out the origin and nature of expressions in Irish, and spent long periods helping students and others in elucidating difficult points of idiom and grammar, but always did so with patience and with a genial sense of humour. It goes without saying that he solved my problems with the Iveragh poets for me and gave me much additional information besides. He was particularly interested in the artistic image of the poets, and it took me no length of time to realize that the reason for this lay in his own creative temperament. He spoke of Irish poets and scholars of the past – especially of Aodhagán Ó Rathaille, Eoghan Rua Ó Súilleabháin and Tomás Rua Ó Súilleabháin – as if he knew them personally; and, indeed, so well did he himself embody that great tradition that it would not be entirely untrue to say that he did know them. They were neighbours of his in the realm of lore and legend, of verse and imagery, just as were his neighbours of the contemporary world such as the rhetorical speaker Fionnán Ó Siochrú from Dún Ghéagáin and the magnificent storyteller Dónall Ó Murchú from Rinn Ruaidh. To a young student of Irish tradition, such people opened up new vistas at the same time as they offered age-old insights into the heritage of Ireland.

Like Fionn MacCumhaill in the heroic sagas, Michael

was a man with knowledge of the past, of the present and of the future. He took a special interest in his family history and could tell of how relatives found themselves on different sides in the American Civil War, as well as how at home they managed to survive the tyranny of landlords and the famines and other vicissitudes of history in the south-west of Ireland. He could go back further. Aware of how the Ua Ciarmhaic sept originated as Eoghanacht kings at Cnoc Áine Cliach (Knockainey in County Limerick), he often speculated on how several of them ended up towards the western Atlantic. He once wrote a letter to me describing an *aisling* or vision that he had one night, when he dreamed that he was back in County Limerick as king of all the rich landscape of the Golden Vale of Munster. He did this of course with a puckish sense of humour, knowing that I was a native of that area, but two aspects of the letter were significant. Firstly, he was reiterating the old Munster tradition of a poet being vouchsafed a vision, and secondly the letter was written entirely in verse and after the revered old style. Much of the appeal of Michael as a *literatus* was this understanding that everything must be done with style and panache, and that it must echo the inherited cultural values from past ages.

But he was also a man of the present. He showed this through his poetry, short stories and novellas; and in equal degree through his many radio broadcasts and television appearances. In these he demonstrated originality and independence of mind, and his genial presence captivated and influenced the hearers. Books came from him in a steady flow. In Irish he wrote *Cliathán na Sceilge* (1984), *Íochtar Trá* (1985), *An Gabhar sa Teampall* (1986), *Barra Taoide* (1988), *Ríocht na dTonn* (1989), *Ceol Maidí Rámha* (1990), *Iníon Keevac* (1996) and

Guth ón Sceilg (2000). Parts of these works have been repeatedly anthologized and broadcast on radio. Then there were the two very valuable collections of his works in English, *Skelligside* (1990) and *Skelligs Calling* (2003), that gained an even wider readership and established him as a leading writer in a county noted for its leading writers. His books were widely and favourably reviewed, literary prizes were awarded to him, and he was fêted and celebrated, yet he never changed. He remained to the end the true writer, humble and creative and always seeking to hone his art to greater achievement.

He numbered among his friends some of the leading poets, writers, artists, and scholars of twentieth-century Ireland, influencing them by his measured approach to culture and his inspired view of his native place. The cassette-tape of his lore, entitled *Chuireas Mo Líonta*, appeared in 1992 and was an immediate success, being highly valued for the material and as the record of the speaking voice of one of the Gaeltacht areas richest in lore down to our own time. Especially popular was the television documentary on Michael and his life and interests entitled *The Goat in the Temple* (1995) – here he made use of an old proverb that became very popular with him and which is the nearest he ever got to satirizing human failings. '*Má théann an gabhar sa teampall,*' he would remark, '*ní stadfaidh sé go haltóir,*' meaning 'If the goat goes into the temple he will not stop until he reaches the altar.' This he used in the title of the book in Irish in which he expressed opinions on a wide variety of subjects. The title draws attention to the sometimes crude contemporary world, which Michael lamented just as much as he welcomed; the increased scope for young people to express their opinions and play their full part in social and cultural affairs.

For Michael was also a man of the future, a factor that is especially evident in his great affection for and championing of the environment. In this regard, *Ríocht na dTonn* is a little masterpiece, simple in description, yet deep and significant in the knowledge and detail, both linguistic and biological, that has gone into it. Very few other people in the Ireland of our time have had such a minute knowledge of the sea, of its plants, birds and fishes. Michael was an expert fisherman, but was also a great lover of all living things and combined the lot in the mind of the humanist and of the artist. He was unflinching in drawing attention to the natural beauty around us – a trait not surprising, one might say, in a native of such a beautiful and colourful part of Ireland, except that Michael possessed such a trait in so full a measure. His family recall the great joy in growing up with such a father, how he brought them on nature excursions by land and sea, how he drew their attention to the continuous changes in colour and mood of the environment, and the example he showed by his under-standing of and affection for the various creatures. Like all people of culture, he was a keen observer of things and of events, many of which happen only in the wilder-ness and far from ordinary human eyes. In his final years, he enjoyed very much feeding the robins that came at his whistle in wintertime, and in the summer he watched carefully for the bees and butterflies that seemed to find particular pleasure in landing on his straw hat.

People from all over the world used to stop and have the most amazing conversations with Michael, and he continued to entertain even when age and failing health was causing him some distress. They would come just to talk, more usually to learn, to buy one of his paintings, or have him sign a copy of one of his books. Often he would dispense with the formalities and just give a painting or a book as a present to a visitor. In his own spare time, he would do some gardening or chat to his family or to neighbours, all of whom understood well that he was a special person, akin to the fine Irish poets and scholars of old and yet with a very modern perspective. Otherwise, he was continually reading: science books, novels, poetry, essays, biographies and books on history. He took a particular interest in travel books, and from these and from his many visitors, as well as his own brief experience abroad, he knew and sensed so much that he was a genuine cosmopolitan in feeling and sentiment.

I have many heart-warming memories of Michael, beginning with the welcome he and Peig gave to me when I first arrived in Ballinskelligs, followed by his in-depth description of the surroundings and the traditional life of land and sea, and progressing into his recitation by heart of reams of poetry and discussion in the grand old style of one proverb after another until late into the night. I remember also his gentle teasing some years later when he realized that I met my future wife Caitríona while holidaying in Ballinskelligs, and later visits of his to Dublin – especially for a painful eye-operation – when in the Gaelic League Club on Harcourt Street he assured us that suffering did not matter to him so long as he was among friends. I remember especially the day that Peig and himself were unexpected but most welcome visitors to the Folklore Department at University College Dublin, on which occasion he presented me with tapes of all his stories, recorded in the most charming Irish.

Fondest of all memories is a more recent one, when his family told me that his wife Peig was sorting out his effects and came upon a memorial card in his wallet. It was the memorial card of my father, who had died in 1982. I had given it to Michael at that time, and he had kept it by him ever since. The two men never met, but they had one distant thread binding them. Both had a connection with Knockainey – my father, an athletic little man, had come there from Kilkenny to train racehorses; Michael, a great big man, was descended from a remote ancestor who had left Knockainey to wrestle with Manannán's horses in the sea. I am sure that they would have had an affinity with each other, and that they have met and discussed many things in an afterlife in which they both, like myself still, firmly believed.

Michael had a great love of the sea and a keen interest in boats and ships of all kinds, being particularly proud of the one-sail fishing boat that he used in his youth and that held special memories for him. He was an expert seaman, and even in advanced years could navigate the dangerous sea-passage to Skellig Michael, the place of the strange but wonderful old monks that he glowed in describing. In this, as in other matters, his recall of scenery and situation was impressive. Such a clear brain made him an excellent farmer and fisherman, but it also made him an expert judge of words. Every word of his – mingling with the imagery that illumined his thought – called forth a phrase, a proverb, a verse, a story.

Of his works, my mind still revolves upon one of the simplest of all the pieces, an item that nevertheless has a resounding meaning for human life in all its contexts. This is his Irish translation of a beautiful little poem, 'Time', which – looking back now – is always increasing in poignancy. I beg to quote it in its entirety and then to give my own translation. [The original English poem also appears at the end of *Skelligside* – ed.]

Gol agus suan im naíonán dom
– am ró-bhuan.
Garsún gáireach cainteach umhal
– am ag siúl.
Cuisle an fhir im chorp ag crith
– am ag rith.
Fáirbrí aois, dronn agus preiceall
– am ag eiteall.
Is gearr go mbead fé scáth na lice
– am imithe.

Cries and sleep as I am a baby
– time too eternal.
A boy laughing, garrulous and obedient
– time is moving.
The man's pulse quivering in my body
– time is running.
Wrinkles of age, stoop and double chin
– time is flying.
Soon I will be under the shadow of the flagstone
– time is gone.

C'est la vie, we might say, but it is my great pleasure to introduce to readers a fine selection of his work. It is a miscellany, a form of writing in which he excelled and that is in accord with his own speaking voice, relaying the variety of tradition and all the while interpreting it with a keen eye. This is the distinguishing mark of Michael, a vigorous prose and contemplative poetry that teeters between tradition and the individual talent. It is very much a nostalgic record of the past, and many people will value it for that, but it also contains within it flashes of inspiration that are at one with universal art. Michael may have been the last of his type in Iveragh. In a sense – given the breadth of his interests – he was the only of his type, but most of all he was a really nice man, a sincere and enlightened one. And that surely is the finest tribute of all that can be paid to a writer.

Dáithí Ó hÓgáin, Associate Professor, Irish Folklore,
University College Dublin

*Cobh, 30 January 1930: Michael Kirby
standing, Michael Moran seated to left,
David Fitzgerald to right of photograph.*

Skelligs Sunset

INTRODUCTION

I am thankful for the simple gifts: the ability to see, hear and observe the things of nature, the rocks, bogs, meadows, sand and seashore of my native place, including birds and animals. All these I took for granted. My people were and still are, thankfully, just simple folk. We were part of the plan of nature. Whether the day was wet or dry, stormy or fine, people in general said: 'Thank God.'

Now in my last two years, trying to finish a century, I humbly attempt to describe nature. Nature is beautiful, bountiful, fearfully awe-inspiring and mysteriously enigmatic. One part of nature's scene has held a special fascination for me: the ever-changing sequence of cloud formation. During my many years as a fisherman I developed an admiration for the arch of the sky during sunrise and sundown. I believe, in my heart and soul, that no human artist can ever emulate patterns that become visible in the embryo of pristine nature.

It was eventide, a light, lazy, rolling swell covered the darkening blue of the sea, reaching westwards to the horizon; a perfect setting for a spectral and ethereal display. Suddenly, the great star stood poised momentarily on the line where the arch of the firmament meets the ocean. Molten rivers of fire streamed upwards like raised arms in adoration, in its centre a blinding whiteness. My mundane thoughts suffered a severe jolt that evening. I could only think of the Transfiguration of Jesus: 'His face did shine as the sun.' (Matt. 17: 2)

The sea between Skellig Michael and Bolus Head became an undulating pathway of sparkling golden light, swaying and shimmering. The clouds took on a wondrous array of colour. In the background, white cumuli thunderheads kept rising like snow-clad peaks whose valleys and gorges filled with complementary hues. Some clouds resembled angry bearded prophets. One dappled brown cloud resembled a baboon holding its monkey-like grey-faced offspring in a protective embrace. The last rays of the sinking star tinted the clouds with roseate pink and yellow kisses before departing. Turning, I could only say: 'Thanks be to God!'

MICHAEL KIRBY
FEBRUARY 2004

SCHOOLDAYS: TUG OF WAR IN THE CLASSROOM

Fond memories pass through my mind, making mental pictures of the past, my early boyhood and most of all my school days and companions.

Ballinskelligs National School for boys and girls opened in 1867, employing four teachers and consisting of two separate adjoining schools for male and female within the one building. My name was entered on the school roll in 1911 at the early age of five years. My only book was called *The First Book*, and it contained little words like 'at', 'cat', 'bat', 'rat' and so on. I do not remember other books. I heard my parents speak of a book called the Readamaidaisy or *Reading Made Easy*, which was its proper title. Another book called *The Three Rs* they called Readin', 'Ritin' and 'Rithmitic.

I remember being transferred from infant grade to first class. I now possessed a lovely small paper table-book that I soon learned to sing like a song: 'One and one is two, two and two is four,' and so on. The teacher helped me to write, showing me how to balance the pencil between the forefinger and the thumb, by placing his open palm over my small hand, guiding my pencil across the page and forming the contour of my first letters. Gaelic lettering was different, having more tails. I found the contrast between Irish and English scripts a bit confusing. I had no difficulty in understanding Gaelic, it being our most used language at home and in the workplace.

Our principal teacher was not a native Irish speaker, making communication with his native-speaking class more difficult and perhaps a little ridiculous from the pupil's point of view. Looking back over that period of my life with what modern jargon terms hindsight, I have come to realize that our teachers had difficulty in dealing with us. They referred to our natural behaviour with such names as 'ignorant rustics, lunatics and clowns', often softening the blow by declaring that the clown was the smartest man in the circus. It must be said, in all fairness to our teachers, that we were the uneducated product, given to them to mould in our formative years into something of value – a formidable task by any standard.

The attendance reached 120 boys at Ballinskelligs National School, a large rural population coming from a congested district area where the average acreage of a smallholding was six to twelve acres. Large native-speaking families were living in poverty-line conditions. Our family owned one milch cow on six acres of cut-away bog. Among many more like us, we did not pity ourselves, but just accepted what we were born into. As a school-goer, I was totally devoid of logical thought as to what the future held or might hold for me. We stayed in school until we were confirmed; after that our future was bleak. We could be classified by the Church as perfect Christians but in digging a ditch the necessary qualifications amounted to a strong back and a weak mind.

Our teacher, a squat, square figure of mellowing bachelorhood, instilled fear into his pupils. He always kept a stockpile of strong hazel birches in the press or locker, and was brutally cruel in his administration of punishment. I witnessed stalwart youths who stood erect with outstretched palms, never flinching from each thudding, swishing cut of the strong hazel birch. I can still see the pallor of agonizing pain from fierce cuts across each open palm being endured manfully. I watched the teacher's face grow pale and deadly serious, as if he really meant to reduce his helpless victim to a mere human wreck, such was his expression of fury. In latter years, I read of the birch being used on convicts, but in our school you daren't miss your homework.

Our school had a goodly supply of open rat holes because of its wooden floors. We formed a conspiracy that at every chance available to us, the hazel rods would be pushed into the rat-hole cavities beneath the floor. 'Operation Rat Hole' seemed to succeed for a time, much to the bewilderment of the teacher. Then one day the brewing storm broke, and a long, latent fury spilled over. This happened when the last hazel rod mysteriously vanished; schoolwork was suspended in the main classroom. Our teacher ordered 'Silence and attention!' while he stood behind the old rostrum, which looked very like the magistrate's desk in the local courtroom. Calling the boys in turn, he questioned each in a low tone regarding the disappearance of the rods.

When the enquiry produced only angelic innocence, the teacher decided on mass punishment for the whole class: ten strokes, five on each palm. But where would he find a suitable rod? Ah, a broom handle! The sweeping brooms had long, rounded, polished handles. Choosing one, he extracted it from the socket of the broom. The first boy to receive his baptism from the heavier weapon withstood the ordeal with valour, grinning at the master through a mask of near laughter and pain, seeming only to infuriate the administrator; whereupon the broom handle snapped into two nearly equal parts, giving the wielder much more control of balance and stroke. We all received our reward for taking part in 'Operation Rat Hole', and it was only a matter of time before we became strong and perfect Christians.

Another form of punishment meant the curtailment of our recreational period prescribed by the Department of Education. The master would keep the senior class involved in maths within the school while he leisurely examined copies. This curtailment of our freedom seemed to hurt more than corporal punishment.

A number of boys suffered from speech impediments. One particular boy who had a most severe speech problem was constantly at loggerheads with the master, who was convinced he could cure the boy's stammer by holding his head high and making him sing the words as he read them. Each day's session of the master's speech therapy and vocal cord exercises ended in disaster. The boy became more and more emotionally conscious of his problem and dreaded each session of speech training. The master could be heard shouting in a loud voice: 'Sing it, you clown! Out with it!'

'The night was dark and dreary ... ah ... bup ... bup!'

'Out with it!'

One day the boy – let's call him John – decided he had to fight back. He grabbed hold of the hazel stick, then started a tug o' war. In the ensuing struggle, the master's spectacles became dislodged, bringing the bout to a sudden end. The master ordered John to get back to his seat. Relations remained strained from then on, until one day hostilities broke out again because John was slow at mathematics. This time he refused to extend his hand for the usual punishment. The master prepared for the fury by removing his spectacles, but he did not reckon with John's next move. The master always wore a heavy gold chain, complete with bar and ornate medallion, looped across his waistcoat. On the chain was his heavy silver watch. I am sure he was proud of this fine piece of jewellery as I often saw him fondle the beautiful chain and subconsciously run it through his fingers. Grabbing John by the arm, the master asked him once more to hold out his hand, but more quickly John grabbed a loop of the gold chain and started to pull. In astonishment the teacher dropped the birch, saying: 'Oh! No, no, Johnny, go back to your seat.' Replacing his glasses, peace was restored. On another occasion the master made the observation that Johnny was, by nature of his impediment, 'a very highly strung person'. But Johnny was the only boy in our class who was logical enough to know that attack was the better part of defence.

We all paid a few pence twice a year towards 'stationery money'. This helped pay for copybooks, pencils and writing pens with red wooden handles mounted with steel nib and holder. We also contributed towards the winter fuel. Each pupil brought two sods (bricks) of turf peat each morning until the fuel store was full. The master made sure that each pupil contributed his fair share.

Looking back, my school days seemed to belong to the Stone Age, down to the blue-black slates we used instead of copybooks, with pencils of the same material. Each two pupils were compelled to stand back-to-back to prevent copying. We would sometimes whisper words or figures to each other. The slate slabs went out with the advent of the copybook and the wooden writing pen and nib.

Christian Doctrine involved learning about our faith in both English and Gaelic. We had no Bible, except for short lessons in Bible history and explanatory catechism. The Bible seemed to be for the more enlightened, or rather smacked of Protestantism. We were not allowed partake in Protestant rituals, funerals, etc. Marrying a Protestant would require a dispensation from the pope. The rules were very strict.

I remember one occasion when the parish priest visited our school in the run-up to confirmation. He took the senior class for a short examination while the teacher stood aside. The purpose of his visit was to find out how we would answer questions on faith and morals when confronted by the bishop. The questions centred on the Ten Commandments. All went well until the sixth commandment: 'Thou shalt not commit adultery.' One by one we were asked what constituted adultery. We did not have a clue. One boy suggested it had to do with a woman. Another gave him some ridiculous answer, whereupon the priestly catechist lost his cool and, folding up his broad-leafed, soft felt hat into a baton-like weapon, proceeded to lambaste us, his budding Christians, about the ears. When the priest had departed the teacher tried to unravel the hitherto unexplained mystery of adultery in the following vague manner: 'Supposing a girl was on her way over the hill and a man met her in a lonely place and knocked her down with the intention of committing adultery ...' All went well until confirmation day. The good bishop grew a little tired after he had examined several classes. He ordered a canon to finish the examination. A boy from our group was asked what was covered by the sixth commandment, to which he answered: 'If a girl was coming over a hill, Father, and a man knocked her down ...'

'Very good, my child! God bless you.'

He then went on to another child, much to the relief

of all concerned.

We were issued with copybooks that cost only a penny each and carried a beautiful specimen headline in perfect copperplate writing, bearing such captions as: 'All that glitters is not gold', 'Discretion is the better part of valour' and 'The darkest hour is that before the dawn', which we would try to imitate by writing the sentence repeatedly until near-perfection was attained. I had trouble with the bottom loop of the letter 'f', which remains added to my legacy of human imperfections. Even to the present moment, I carry with me a most vivid recollection of receiving a violent blow with an open palm, which thereby compressed the air within my eardrum, causing searing pain and deafness that I never revealed to my parents because of a fear on my own part. The violence and sudden impact of the blow seems like a happening of yesterday.

Watches were only for rich people, anchored within breast pockets with gold or silver chains, and looped across the noble breasts of lawyers, churchmen, tavern keepers, doctors, teachers and landlords. The first German alarm clocks appeared in the shop fronts of Cahersiveen in the first decade of the last century. Their prices ranged from two-and-six to five shillings. The school clock stood in an elevated position on top of the tall press built into the wall. The clock was manufactured in the USA by the Ansonia Clock Company in New Haven, Connecticut. It replaced the old clock with weights and chains and had a spring-wound mechanism that struck the hours. The master adjusted the time by moving the hands backwards or forwards, by reaching up with a long stick kept for that purpose.

Our senior class consisted of some very bright, mischievous boys who decided to set the clock forward by five minutes while the master accompanied the parish priest to the school gate, where the two would stand discussing matters in private. That evening we closed school five minutes earlier than usual. Pranks like this went on until the master became suspicious and decided to take action. He left the schoolroom, apparently to inspect the latrines situated at the rear of the school. Tom Sullivan, a very fine strapping lad, stepped up to the rostrum and, wielding the long stick, proceeded to adjust the hands of the clock at least fifteen minutes ahead. Suddenly, a loud, tapping noise attracted our attention, and the master's scowling face appeared at the back of the window with a wagging finger. Tom Sullivan scampered back to his seat in expectation of severe punishment. When he entered the room all our eyes focused on the master who, to our astonishment, stood before the class smiling broadly. He called on Tom Sullivan to come forward. Tom approached the master with trepidation and was asked the question: 'Now, Tom did you interfere with the clock?'

'I did, sir!'

'Why?'

'For you to let us home early, sir!'

'By how many minutes did you alter the clock, Tom?'

'Fifteen minutes, sir!'

The master glanced at his pocket watch and looked in turn at the school clock. 'Exactly, Tom! Now go back to your seat and I will give you a set of problems to occupy your time for an extra fifteen minutes, and every time the clock is interfered with, you will stay in school until you change your ways!'

That was the last time we interfered with the new school clock. The master had won that round. He had his good points as well, like the little girl in the poem:

'When she was good, she was very, very good, but when she was bad, she was horrid.'

It is sad to think that the old school clock with its weights and chains has lost its place with the maelstrom of the rapid advance in modern technology. It is now a museum exhibit of the not-so-distant past. No longer does it wag its pendulum like a welcoming, faithful canine greeting its master, or emit a leisurely, soothing tick-tock, tick-tock. Now only a small battery inserted within its interior controls the almost empty space. No winding key is required anymore. For a piece that emerged from the shadow of the sun cast on a beauti-fully engraved rock in a rich man's garden, I mourn your passing. They left you with no guts to live.

We contributed threepence each towards a leather football that cost twelve shillings. The master contributed four shillings. He kept the inflated ball in the school-room. He acted as referee and organized inter-school games. He also gave physical drill instruction in the school. He was a very good music teacher. We liked the way he used a steel tuning fork to find the note. He taught us many songs, in both Gaelic and English, and we had an excellent school choir.

At a later date our football became a source of annoyance to the teacher. Because of our playground being in close proximity to Seamus O'Leary's oat field, the ball would occasionally soar over the boundary fence. It would become lost for a while among the yet green, unripened crop of standing oat stalks. A number of boys would go over to retrieve the ball. Owing to the damage to his oat crop created by repeated trampling, O'Leary, having given several warnings, decided he must take some action.

One day, when class had resumed after our play

hour, we were all engrossed in various tasks. Suddenly, the door swung violently open, revealing the form of a wild, dishevelled man standing like a pillar of salt in the doorway, shirt sleeves folded to the elbow, with a gorilla-like chest, pale and unshaven face, a hook nose and greying tangle of once-dark, bedraggled hair falling around his ears. Standing there with a reaping hook in hand, his leering eyebrows and his fierce blue eyes seemed to penetrate the room. Our teacher rushed towards him saying: 'Oh, no, no! You can't enter the school, James! Please go at once!' The master found himself suddenly pushed aside and into a corner by Seamus who spoke in Gaelic, saying, '*Má chuireann tú lámh orm, bainfidh mé an ceann díot!*' ('If you put a hand on me, I'll cut your head off!') while making a looping gesture with the reaping hook. Turning towards the class, he spied a little heap of peat sods near the fireplace and proceeded to pelt us with fury. We all dived for cover beneath our desks. The map of Europe hung on the back wall. One peat sod landed on the shores of the Black Sea, leaving a little crater in the grain-growing regions of the Ukraine. O'Leary, having vented his fury, gave a strong warning in Gaelic before departing: if we caused any further damage to his crop, he would return.

The master arranged with the assistant teacher, who owned a small farm not far from the school premises, to let us play football in his property, thereby avoiding any further contact with O'Leary, who in all fairness had suffered much loss to his oat crop.

As a matter of interest, the aggrieved Seamus O'Leary, my friend and next-door neighbour, was the last surviving member of the O'Leary family who were cruelly evicted and brutally treated by the Crown forces when the last eviction took place in south Iveragh, County

Kerry, in the year 1864.

Our teacher grew beautiful geraniums in red clay pots. He would send us out on the roadway to collect a bucket of fresh horse droppings. To these we added water, pounding and mixing until it dissolved into a rich dark-brown liquid, which the master poured into a beaker jug. This solution was used very effectively as a fertilizer to grow a fine crop of geraniums. No doubt medics today would shrink in horror at handling horse manure without protection.

Some schoolbooks, both in Gaelic and English, were wonderfully informative and interesting. A Gaelic book entitled *An Treas Leabhar* had some beautiful Gaelic poems like 'Bán Chnoic Éireann Ó' ('The Fair Hills of Erin') and 'An Díbirtheach ó Éirinn'.

Tháinig chun an taoide díbirtheach ó Éirinn ...

There came to the beach a poor exile of Erin,
The dew on his thin robe was heavy and chill,
For his country he sighed when at twilight repairing,
To wander alone by a wind-beaten hill.

The Gaelic prose was precise and difficult for the country boy who came from a native Irish-speaking fireside. There appeared to be a wide gap between the Gaelic he listened to at home and that which he was obliged to read from the school reader, which bore the imprimatur of the academy.

I do not wish to find fault with high standards, and only relate a factual experience of my school days. The English readers had many beautiful essays and poems. The last book we were introduced to was *Macbeth*, and we read it aloud. Connie Curran, Paddy Connor and I read the parts of the three witches. I was the first witch. I remember we would read it in turn. We had already devoured the long poem, *The Rime of the Ancient Mariner*. There were so many verses in it to learn by rote. The first night I brought it home I left the book down out of my hands and our young pup chewed it. Two other unusual books we had were *Around the World in Eighty Days* and *Twenty Thousand Leagues Under the Sea*.

Elementary science was taught in the year or two before we left school. There was a grant given for the teaching of rural science. I had a special love for chemistry.

After confirmation, further education seemed futile. We could read and write and do a few simple problems in maths, and had a fair, general knowledge of geography, natural science and poetry.

The secondary school was situated in Cahersiveen, staffed by Christian Brothers who were established there before the turn of the century. That school was out of bounds. We had no means of transport. Our parents could not afford to pay for digs in Cahersiveen and bicycles were non-existent. Some boys were fortunate to have relatives in America who sent passage money for the New World. The classes that had attended Ballinskelligs National School during the end of the nineteenth century could sit for the King's scholarship. Many became engineers in the Colonial Service and served in responsible posts in India, Malaysia and Argentina. One was chief of police in Malaysia, one in charge of the grain stores in Buenos Aires and another a major in the British army in India. Many more became rich men in Canada, the United States of America, Australia and New Zealand. This goes to show that the Irish peasantry had brains to burn, but the opportunity for work or employment did not exist.

All my boyhood school companions have gone to

their reward. The majority rest in foreign soil, where they found employment and threw in their lot with others for better or worse. Gone also are our teachers, who in our best interests had the unenviable task of trying to fit us for at least a menial part in the emerging society of this country. May they rest in peace.

Sadly, the schoolhouse is now closed.

Voices of Valentia

This poem is dedicated to P.J. Reardon, a native of Valentia, who was married to my sister Mamie. They lived in Hamden, Connecticut, USA. The poem first appeared in The Voices of Valentia *published in 1972–3.*

Voices of youth, I hear you calling,
Phantom voices from the distant past.
Voices that now fill me with a longing,
Island voices, tearing at my heart.

I hear again the moaning of the sea surf,
The whistle of the maybird on the moor,
The creaking carts are bringing home the brown turf,
A mother's home call from an evening door.

I hear the seine boats coming up the harbour
The dipping and the swinging of the oars,
The old stone pier is loud with work and laughter,
As fisherfolk unload the silvery store.

Above Ceann Brí I hear the raucous raven,
On towering cliff, where wheeling sea birds go
To the lamenting seal in its blue haven,
Safe in the echoing caverns far below.

And last of all I hear the south wind ringing,
A-bringing sea-wrack to the Cave of Calves.
No wonder that an exile's thoughts go winging
To the Island voices tearing at my heart.

SEÁN Ó CONAILL: KING OF THE STORYTELLERS

Seán Ó Conaill was born in 1853 in the village of Cill Rialaig and it was there he died on 21 May 1931. His home was among a cluster of cosy, white-walled, thatched cottages, nestling beneath the shelter of the rugged and majestic crag that looms overhead on the road to Bolus. At one time there were eleven little cottages in all, each house carefully situated with its back to the storm and its face to the rising sun, giving an extended panoramic view to native or tourist, a view such as Brian Merriman portrays for us in his Gaelic composition in verse, *Cúirt an Mheán Oíche* (*The Midnight Court*):

Do ghealadh an croí, a bheadh críonn le cianta.

It would gladden the heart of the old or weary.

It was into this beautiful setting that Seán Ó Conaill was delivered and it remained his birthright until the day he died. Beneath his feet lay the clear, unpolluted waters of Ballinskelligs Bay. At night he could hear the moaning of the surf in Cuas na Léime, the cave where, it is said, a fugitive escaped capture from Cromwell's forces by taking a flying leap across the neck of its narrow span. One could stand on the roadway outside Seán's house and cast a stone into the sea below.

Is it any wonder that Seán became king of the storytellers, inspired by the historical Gaelic place names, going back to Mo Ruth, Árd Rí na nDraoithe, the high king of the magicians, whose summer residence was in Béal Inse, Oileán Dairbhre (Valentia). He had only to look south to feast his eyes on the towering Teach Uí Dhuinn, House of Don, son of Milesius, later known as the Bull Rock lighthouse, together with the Calf and the Cow nearby, to which Tomás Rua Ó Súilleabháin makes reference in a little poem where he says in Gaelic:

Tá an Sceilg is an Scairbh Thiar 'na seasamh,
An Bhó 's an Tarbh taobh leo,
An Lao go blasta nár ól riamh bainne,
Is ard a's is garbh ghéimeann.

Skelligs and Scariff are westward standing,
The Cow and Bull lie near them,
And a Calf that never drank of milk,
How loud and tough its bellow.

Seán was a man of dignity who had a huge respect for the oral tradition of our noble ancestry. He valued his culture and his heritage. Professor Séamus Delargy from University College, Dublin visited him in Cill Rialaig and transcribed a wealth of stories from the lips of the great *seanchaí,* and published them in *Leabhar Sheáin Í Chonaill.*

Séamus Delargy was a scholar and master linguist, refined, elegant and gentlemanly, who held the chair of Roinn Béaloideas na hÉireann in UCD. It was his first visit to Kerry in 1923 when he attended an Irish summer course for national teachers in Caherdaniel. From there he visited Ballinskelligs and met with Fíonán Mac Coluim, a founder member of Conradh na Gaeilge, and old John Harty, a man known to all as Seana Sheáin. John was a native Irish speaker and a lover of the Irish tongue who was now retired from his job in South America where he was superintendent of a cable station for Western Union.

Fíonán and Seana Sheáin helped the professor make his first contact with the great mine of folklore that was Seán Ó Conaill. The fine scholar who had visited and lectured in many lands knew immediately he had discovered the untapped mother-lode of a great *seanchaí*'s mind. A natural storyteller, he loved to relate exploits of a hero or a family; tales of pre-Christian Ireland or long sagas of perhaps Nordic flavour or a mixture of Greek mythology; tales of Fionn and the Fianna, of great feasts and the chase of the wild boar or the fleet-footed fawn; beautiful tales of King Conor Mac Neasa, 'when the stream ran white', and tales of Queen Maeve, the Táin Bó Cuailnge and Cúchulainn; tales that astonished the learned professor.

Seán Ó Conaill loved the beauty of his art. It was said of him that as an old man cowherding on the furzy slopes of his native Cill Rialaig he could be heard speaking in a loud voice verses from some poem, or speaking lines from one of his many favourite tales of the past. The *seanchaí* admitted to having no approved education, except two weeks in a hedge school, gaining from life his knowledge of nature and how to survive on a few bleak stony acres perched high on the cliff top overlooking Ballinskelligs Bay.

A small farmer and fisherman, he tilled the most fertile strips between the rocks, as did his neighbours, on a patchwork of small fields. The little grey donkey with the pannier baskets, wooden straddle and *srathar fhada* – straw mattress – was the workhorse who transported the kelp and farmyard manure to the field on the hill. The potato beds were prepared with the long iron spade, a slow and arduous task requiring time and patience. The *sciolláns* or split potatoes, each with two eye sprouts, were laid on a bed of farmyard manure and covered with a generous layer of broken clay. What more rewarding sight on a balmy May evening than the lush green potato beds under full blossom, and better still, to dig the flowery shrubs with clusters of ripening potatoes clinging to their roots on St John's Eve!

Dr Delargy wrote of Seán Ó Conaill as having a wide knowledge of natural things: the phases of the moon, the spring tides, herbal medicines and a vocabulary of thousands of words in Gaelic. Weaving his tales, he could hold his listeners spellbound with his soft, gentle voice. He was always in complete command, confidently natural. The professor would say that, like the wayfarer in William Wordsworth's poem 'The Old Cumberland Beggar', he possessed 'a thing more precious far than all that books …'.

The *seanchaí* tells of hearing most of his tales from his ancestors by the hearthstones of his neighbours. Only needing to hear a story once, he could retain it, stored in his memory forever. He tells of a time he visited a neighbouring townland where he listened to a storyteller from another parish who told a certain old tale that Seán did not have in his stock. The night rained in torrents and became very stormy, and Seán waited anxiously for the story to finish, owing to the fact of having to cross a swollen stream in the darkness. He relates his ordeal of trying to negotiate the billowing torrent by making a desperate leap and, failing to reach the far bank, he plunged into the water, thereby losing his headgear. On reaching home he stood in the doorway, bareheaded, dishevelled and dripping wet. His good wife Cáit exclaimed in amazement: '*A Thiarna, a*

Sheáin, a chroí, cad a bhain duit?' meaning, 'Lord, Seán! What happened to you?' Whereupon Seán replied: *'Chailleas mo chaipín, ach thugas liom mo scéal!'* ('I only lost my cap but I brought home my story!')

The professor visited my father on many occasions when he brought several large maps of the coastline from Kenmare to Dingle Bay, showing the various indentations, caves, islands, reefs, headlands, points, beaches, cliffs, etc. The maps were the property of the Ordnance Survey office. My father supplied the Gaelic place names, while Delargy wrote them into their correct places on the map. Several of those names were in very old Gaelic, beautiful names like Cuas Elinore, Elinore's Cave – I never heard the story of Elinore – and Boilg Anders, Ander's Rock; names that link us with the Fianna and the Milesians, like An Carraig Oisín, Oisín's Rock, Carraig Éanna, Eanna's Rock; and names like Ceann Aonaigh, The Headland of the Aonaig, Bosca an Pheidléara, The Pedlar's Box, Leac an Loiscreáin, The Burning Flagstone, and Leac a' Phriosúin, The Prison Rock. Many hundreds of place names he identified that the professor himself found difficult to unravel.

I spoke with the learned master on the telephone a short time before he died. He talked to me about Ballinskelligs and Cill Rialaig in loving terms, of the great wealth of folklore he found there and the grand old *Gaeilgeoirí* he met. It was his intention to return to Cill Rialaig again. Seán had assured him that the source of the crystal spring had not run dry and that a new set of stories was already taking possession of his mind. Little did Dr Delargy imagine that this would be the last time he was to spend an evening in the company of the man he had learned to admire so much! A man who had no English and did not understand the language of the

Sassanach, Seán Ó Conaill never used coarse or vulgar language, and was always gentle in the delivery of his vast wealth of lore. The last meeting with the gentle Gaelic sage was on Sunday evening, 19 April 1931. I quote from Dr Delargy's own words in Gaelic: 'He walked with me to the gable end of his thatched cottage where he bade me goodbye. Little did I realize it was to be our last meeting. He died a month later, on 21 May 1931.'

Seán and his wife Cáit lie together in Mainistir Mhichíl, Ballinskelligs. Their home is now in ruins, but a limestone plaque marks the site where the king of storytellers once lived.

THE COURTING OF MOLL MOLLOY

Black Moll Molloy was the bane of the rustic young swains who fain would win her affection. Moll remained as far as the male population was concerned the ultimate, feminine enigma. She could be as gentle as a summer zephyr or wild and sweeping as an autumn gale. Her azure eyes were a dyad of blue, a matching of sky and ocean. Her raven tresses wore the dark polish of the sloe on the thorn. She was the dark maid of the glen whom the poets were wont to rave about:

> On the hill I have a cow,
> I have herded it till now,
> Then a dark maiden stole my reason.

The kind that another poet describes in raunchy Gaelic verse:

> A red-haired maiden,
> Will lead the host,
> While the swarthy one
> Is hot and kissing.
> The dark white flower,
> Is my heart's wishing.

Moll remained to one and all as fickle as the blown thistledown, or the snow-white fluff of ripe bog-cotton wafting aloof across the purple turf. To all except one young stripling Paudeen Rua, who could no longer resist the temptation of laying his hands on the wild, unbonded, unbridled filly, singing as she strode airily along, swinging her pail that she would fill from the bubbling spring, whose unending source of pure crystal water emerged from beneath Carraig Bán, overlooking the harbour. As she was about to fill her pail, Paudeen Rua pounced from behind the rock, spun her around and for a fleeting moment held her in tight embrace. His lips were about to touch hers, but so near and yet so far! With a shriek she tore herself loose from his grasp and, as he advanced once more, this time with a lustful grin, dark Moll swung the empty pail with deadly accuracy. The bottom rim made slicing contact with his head. He lay where he fell, a bleeding Adonis, at the feet of the goddess whom he wished to covet. She ran all the way home, meeting her brother who had heard her scream.

'I have killed Paudeen Rua! He is dead! He is dead, up there lying by the spring!'

Tim, her brother, went to investigate, and found Paudeen in a sitting position, holding his head. He was still bleeding profusely from a clean scalp wound, of about six inches, directly over his right ear, where the bottom hoop of Moll's bucket made contact. A fisherman who had also witnessed the drama was laughingly rendering first aid. Moll arrived with some clean linen strips, which her brother had called her to bring at once. Tim said the wound was not very serious, but would require a doctor's attention and maybe a few stitches to draw it together. Paudeen Rua rocked his head from side to side; his exclamations were funny and very unprintable.

'What got into me at all! Sorry, Tim and sorry, Moll! I only wanted to kiss you, honest, but I lost the head! Don't tell the doctor, Tim!'

'Let's say you were shearing sheep and you had an accident,' said Tim.

After a short lapse of time the head wound had healed sufficiently to allow Paudeen to mix in public once more. Despite all the dark secrecy, somebody let the cat escape. Paudeen became a hero, a villain, a Jack the Ripper, a libidinous lover and was chased after by some of the more adventurous females. One old wag said: 'It must have beaten all records for the erection of the shortest duration.'

Dark Moll was the topic of the hour. Some said: 'Shame on Paudeen Rua!' Others went to shocking extremes, adding to the tale in each telling, until it finally bubbled with ruin and ravishing rape. In the meantime Paudeen apologized to Moll and was received by both herself and her brother Tim, much to the surprise of the neighbours, who now turned the tale around. Rumour had it they were to be married, until finally it fizzled out and came to be regarded as an old wives' tale, such as the one that one woman heard another woman say, that old Paddy Smith laid an egg yesterday.

When the last whisper was whispered and discussion became normal once again, it must be said that dark Moll had her own secret lover, hidden deep within her heart, a secret lover she never revealed, but admired from a distance. He was Sean Moore, her neighbour. Sean was an excellent musician and dancer. Moll liked to sit beside him at a crossroads dance and listen to his tunes. Other than that, she never betrayed any emotion by sign, smile or spoken word.

Sean Moore was a boat builder. His trade was handed down to him by his father, who had served his apprenticeship in a Scottish boatyard. The father married a Scottish girl, and brought her to Ireland, where she died soon after their only son was born. Sean was now thirty-two and lived alone since his father's death ten years previously. His little farm consisted of fourteen acres beside the harbour. Seven acres were good land and seven acres comprised jumbled heaps of rock of all shapes and sizes. In Gaelic those rocky fields were called the Claddarach (meaning strewn with great slabs of stone, where the mountain slipped downwards in a great landslide some centuries previously).

Sean's father built a neat cottage overlooking the harbour with three bedrooms, a kitchen and some outoffices. The walls were built of dry stone masonry, each stone carefully set, becoming a perfect joint for the next overlapping stone. The masonry was meant to be admired, such as that found in tales of old about the Gobán Saor, the builder of great castles and churches in early Ireland. The roof was pitch pine that Sean and his father salvaged from the wreck of an old schooner. It was thatched with cut and sewn reed. The inner walls were plastered with lime, cement and sand. The windows were large and airy and the front door was covered with a large slab of slate that sheltered it from the rain. A wall of grey stone surrounded the house, while broad slabs formed a series of easy steps downwards to the white sand. It formed a pretty picture to behold. This was Sean Moore's paradise. He was content to live a life he had accepted as natural, without female intrusion, though he often regretted not having the privilege of a mother to share his parental imbalance.

Lamb Island lay across the harbour like a sleeping giant, consisting of fifteen acres. The north end of the island, being nearer to the mainland, was a narrow channel that became wider at the south entrance. The little harbour was well sheltered in stormy conditions.

The island belonged to Moll's family for centuries. They farmed sheep and fished for salmon long before the landlords and bailiffs took over. They also worked hard at trapping lobster, which were found in abundance.

Moll attended secondary school at the local convent, when at the age of sixteen she became suddenly bereaved. She lost her parents one fine evening in spring. Her father and mother were returning from the mainland market and, as they sailed across the short corner of the inlet close to their own beach, a sudden whirlwind struck the frail craft, which turned keel upwards close to their journey's end. Before help had arrived they were both drowned.

The old adage that trouble never comes alone seemed to hold true. Moll was suddenly called upon to surrender her scholastic career to care for her brother Tim, who had slipped from a cliff ledge when attempting to rescue a sheep, trapped in a position of no return on the treacherous face of Faill a' Deamhain. He was found to be suffering from severe injuries, including a broken hip joint. After his discharge from hospital, he was obliged to use a crutch for many months. He walked with a limp for the rest of his life. Moll had to shoulder the burden of the work until Tim recovered his health. It was now fourteen years since all this happened and Moll's next birthday was coming thirty. Any romantic notions she may have entertained during her teenage years seemed to diminish into mature womanhood, until one night in January there came a turning point in her life and that of her brother.

They were sitting comfortably near the open fire that was throwing a plume of soft, warm flame from the peat heaped on the hearthstone. Tim was putting the finishing touch to the bottom chime of a shapely, curved

lobster pot woven from green osiers grown and culti-
vated in a special grove behind the house. These were
mixed with wild sally twigs. The finished product was a
perfect work of art. Tim was preparing for the coming
lobster season. Moll was repairing a trammel net,
replacing broken meshes and knitting in new portions
where the net had been badly torn, and well able she
was. With swift turns of her wrist she squeezed knots
into place with her needle and twine. A peaceful silence
filled the old kitchen except for the crackling flames,
which leaped and played with the chimney breast.

Tim was first to speak, as he pushed the lobster pot
aside: 'Another new string for the next season, Moll!
We will need another score at least.'

'That was a beautiful pot, Tim!'

'There is something else more important than the
fishing gear. We will go across to see Sean Moore
tomorrow. Our boat needs repair. I will ask him to have
a look at her.'

Moll did not answer at once, but shook her head
slowly before speaking: 'Tim, I always thought you had
great wisdom, but now I know you have a thick skull or
maybe only a tin can with a pebble for a brain. For
God's sake! Can't you see it's not a repair job we need
but a brand new boat.'

'Ah Moll, I say the boat can be repaired. We will let
Sean Moore decide.'

'I know, Tim, what Sean's decision will be. Can't you
see, several of her foot hooks are broken and the dead
woods are rotten. She will need new top timbers, upper
streaks, new gunwales – and a whole lot more. You make
me sick, Tim Molloy, having all the money we have
made from sheep and fishing stashed away in the bank!
No wonder the bank manager shakes your hand and

invites you into the back room whenever you visit him. You are getting on now, Tim! Why are you so miserable about spending a little for the sake of a new boat?'

'Yes Moll, I have a good deal of money, all saved for you. You gave up everything to care for me, when I had only crutches to depend on. You are now thirty years old and I would like you to choose a partner. I will turn all my money over to you when you get married. Where is the use of a new boat without a crew for the future!'

'Ah Tim, you can choose to build a new boat but you can't choose a suitable partner for me and don't dare talk to me about a suitable partner. He is not born yet and his mother is dead. Who will take me to the matchmaker?'

'Enough, Moll! We will go over tomorrow.'

'All right, Tim. One thing at a time, the new boat first.'

Next day they rowed across the sandy channel to the beach in front of Sean Moore's house. It was as if he had expected them. He hurried down the steps to greet them, helped them secure the boat, and invited them up to the house in spite of Tim's protesting that he wished to talk about the business of a new boat. Sean Moore replied: 'This is a cold January day. Let's go up and sit by the fire.'

Moll was very shy and lacked any constructive contribution towards conversation. She seemed overawed by the close presence of the one person she secretly loved. When they entered the kitchen, a fire of bog deal roots, perhaps some thousand of years old, full of oil and resin, blazed on the open hearth.

'Pull up your chairs,' said Sean, 'while I get the bottle and some glasses.'

'No, no!' said Tim. 'We did not come to make a match.'

Moll blushed and said: 'Don't make fun of everything. We came to talk about the boat, Tim.'

'For my part,' said Sean Moore, 'I would rather you came more often. It can be lonely here sometimes. I would like your company and I am not shy to say this house needs the hand of a woman.'

Moll admired the kitchen, where everything was in such proper order and so spotlessly clean. Sean placed a hand on Moll's shoulder, saying: 'Will you do something for us now that you are here, while Tim and myself go down and inspect the boat? Will you make a nice warm cup of tea for us all, with some bacon and egg? I had no dinner, so we are all hungry.' Moll consented readily. Sean showed her a well-stocked larder where the delph was to be had, the frying pan, the kettle and the spring water. 'You'll give us a call when the meal is ready,' said Sean.

Tim and Sean walked to the beach. Tim said: 'I think you have some special power over Moll. Do you see how readily she went to work for you? She usually is not so willing. I think my sister has a soft spot for you.'

'I wish that were so, Tim,' said Sean.

On reaching the beach, Sean produced a pocketknife with a sharp, pointed blade and proceeded to probe every square foot of the old boat. When he had finished he said: 'Tim, you can say "Goodbye, old ship of mine!" I'm sorry. The old lady served you well, but she is now past repairing. In truth, her timbers are soggy and waterlogged. I will lend you my small boat until the new one is ready.'

'As you say, Sean. Moll's judgment was sound.'

'It was your father who built her before you were born. She was a grand boat in a sudden blow. She could nearly trample the waves like a storm witch. I would suggest you give the new boat extra length and six inches more beam.'

'Thank you, Sean. Whatever you say can be only for my good. Shall I give you some of the money for building her now?'

'No, Tim. I will buy the material first. When I have that done I will give you an estimation of how much the boat will cost.'

'What could be more fair.' said Tim. 'I have a question to ask you, but it must be kept a secret.'

'Ask any question you like. Fire away!' said Sean.

'Tell me truly, Sean, did you ever think of taking a wife?'

'I often turned the question over in my mind. The girls I liked I never had the courage to ask, and those who were available I didn't like. Maybe loneliness is better than lovelessness! A man must have a warm spot in his heart for the girl he will choose to live with for the rest of his life. The day of the matchmaker is over, Tim. I don't believe in that anymore. It was like taking a cow to the bull. Who can tell what's under her petticoat or what's inside my trouser for that matter! People should know more about their suitability before tying the knot.'

'Oh I agree. I agree entirely,' said Tim. 'But one more question, Sean. Tell me, would you marry Moll?'

'How can I tell you, Tim, when I do not know her? Moll is a very beautiful girl. Of course I would like her to be my wife.'

'Well, Sean, I am thinking Moll has a sneaking flare for you. All both of you want now is a little bit of encouragement, or maybe a little bit of courting on the sly. You make the boat for me and I'll send a fine spring salmon into your net very soon, but take her gently. Let her have a little bit of her own way for she is as wild as nature itself and don't put a gaff or hook on her too soon.'

'I promise you Tim. I will play my cards and play them well. All I can say now is, one day at a time. Before this boat is finished you will see me buy a golden ring.'

'No statements now, Sean Moore. You gave me your word, so shake hands on it. Hand and word!'

At that moment Moll called to them from the top of the steps.

When they entered, Moll had a nice lunch ready, thin slices of home-cured bacon with fried eggs.

'Ye must both be cold! As a matter of fact, I am hungry also,' said Moll. 'I saw you both shake hands.'

'Yes,' said Tim, 'every bargain is sealed by hand and word.'

'The bargain! What bargain, Tim? We came over to find out about the boat. If it is such a secret bargain, I do not want to know anymore.'

Sean Moore sat next to Moll. He placed his hand gently on Moll's arm.

'Don't worry, there are no secret agreements between us. Everything you said about the boat is true. In fact, the old boat is dangerous. I am letting you have the loan of my small boat until the new one is ready.'

'But Sean, I saw you both shake hands!'

'Yes, Moll. This is how all good bargains are clinched, with hand and word. Won't you shake hands with me, Moll?'

She reached out her hand and Sean squeezed it gently saying: 'No secrets from you Moll! Only for you we would not have this nice meal. This house is badly in need of a woman's hand and a woman's love.'

Moll did not answer, but cast her eyes on the floor, until Tim stood up saying he was going over to the

Claddarach to find some slabs of stone suitable for a fireplace.

'I will wash the dishes,' said Sean.

'I will lend a hand,' said Moll.

When all was tidied, they both sat near the fire. Moll asked when he expected to start on the new boat.

'I would like to build it as soon as possible. I lose almost two hours a day preparing the mid-day meal.'

'I will row over each day at twelve to prepare your dinner,' said Moll.

'That is a wonderful idea,' said Sean.

At that moment Tim entered by the back door. They told him of the new arrangements.

'Very good,' he said. 'And perhaps Moll will help you with the building of the boat as well? She is well able to use the plane and the saw, and can fashion an oar from a spar of rough wood in time of need.'

'That's the best piece of news I have heard from you both!' said Sean Moore. 'I will find plenty of work for her with plane and saw.'

'Will you give it a try, Moll?'

Moll nodded in agreement. Tim knew in his heart if everything went as planned the first of the spring salmon would soon be enmeshed in Sean's net.

Sean Moore bought the necessary wood: the slabs of crooked oak for the floor sticks, ribs and side hooks and a keel of straight-grained black oak, one wide slab for the transom, a special piece for the bow stem and apron, and deadwoods. The plank was of special white deal; thwarts and gunwales were of pine. Sean stored the wood in a long, corrugated-iron shed at the back of the yard. It was here he prepared the keel and made ready for it to be laid.

All the tools were sorted out and sharpened. The

plane irons were taken apart and ground down on the large grindstone and finished on the fine oilstone. All wood-cutting instruments had to have razor-edge sharpness. The jointing planes and short smoothing planes must make a low whistling noise when perfectly sharp. Spoke shaves, drawknives and saws were all cleaned and sharpened. Everything was in readiness to construct the boat. Sean made a scaled drawing. It had new dimensions as he wished to depart from the old traditional method, which had no fixed plan. Sean's father avowed that the best judge of a boat was the water and its behaviour in a turbulent seaway.

Three weeks had elapsed since Tim and Moll decided it was time to pay Sean a visit. Tim sat in the stern of the boat while Moll plied her broad-bladed paddles with even strokes, always reaching ahead for a long stroke, to finish with a neat feathering of the blade. Practise makes perfect, and, having perfect control of the boat, she made it all look so easy to the eye of the amateur. The boat was being steered as if by some unseen helmsman in the direction she wished it to go. She was part of the boat and the boat became part of her.

Sean Moore stood on the beach waiting to receive them. As the bow of the boat touched the soft sand, Moll shipped her oars and jumped over the side while the boat was still in motion. She helped Sean pull the boat clear of the water. Tim left the stern sheet and stepped onto the beach. Sean welcomed them, saying he had been expecting them for some days. Moll and Tim went to the shed where they admired Sean's drawing and the laying of the keel.

'Come,' said Sean. 'We will go inside where it is warmer. This day is very cold. The kettle is steaming, so once more I will ask you to make us some tea. I have been the cook in this house for far too long. I will start work earnestly tomorrow.'

'I will bring over a servant girl tomorrow,' said Tim.

'Stop your gibberish, Tim. It's not as a servant I am coming over but to save time.'

'Don't be so sensitive with me, Moll. Every word I say in fun, you get so serious about.'

'Perhaps you're right, Tim. If I had emigrated I could have had the same job you seem to offer so lightly, and had I emigrated you would have a different tale to tell, and perhaps you would not be as well kept. You were never accustomed to have a soiled shirt on your back.'

'I will leave you both,' said Tim. 'I am going to the Claddarach to get the special stones I want. That place is very interesting. But before I leave, I want to tell you, Moll, that you brought back the words of an old Gaelic song in your reference to the soiled shirt.

> My wife lies in the churchyard,
> Her pillow a cold stone slab.
> And the sign of my sorrow I carry,
> A soiled shirt I wear on my back.'

'Get on with you, Tim, something other than the quest for stones is taking you to the Claddarach!'

'Ah!' exclaimed Tim, before closing the door behind him.

> Three things I know not,
> The belly of a long autumn night,
> The bottom of a newborn babe,
> And the mind of womankind.'

'There is an old folk tale handed down from generation to generation, or said more suitably in Gaelic, *ó ghlúin go glúin*, about how that great heap of stones

37

they call the Claddarach came about,' said Sean.

'What old tale?' said Moll. 'I have never heard a story about that place. Of course it could be without skin, taste or colour, as they say. Please tell me the story, Sean. I love the old ones even if they are part fable.'

'Pull your chair closer to the heat so, Moll, while I get some turf from the rick in the yard.'

Sean brought a full armful of dark hard sods of peat. Moll grasped the long fire tongs with which she opened out the glowing embers, exposing the back of the fireplace. First she placed a row of long square sods against the back wall, like soldiers standing to attention with their boots in the fire. She then replaced all the glowing and half-burned pieces of peat and carefully built up the sides. In no time at all the flames were brightening up the chimney place. Moll was an expert with the tongs. She held it in her right hand, with her forefinger held firmly inside the prongs. She could have plucked a needle from the flames with the clumsy instrument.

'Bring your chair close to mine, Moll. Are you afraid of being alone with me?'

'Sean, don't be ridiculous! You are undoubtedly a big, strong man, but some day before the boat is finished I will challenge you to a wrestling match. But not tonight, as I wish to hear the old tale.'

Pulling her chair close to his side, she said: 'Please start.'

'This is the version,' said Sean, 'that I heard from the lips of my father. What the local people called the Big House stood up there under the hill in a fertile hollow called Clais Bán or the White Hollow. It was there the best land lay and still remains. The estate was the property of a landlord who was both rich and powerful. Some said he was part pirate, and had amassed a great fortune from ill-gotten gain. One of his ears was missing, as if sheared off by a sword cut. He was cross-eyed, with a bald head and a broken nose and was nicknamed Fathach na Súile Cama or Giant of the Crooked Eyes. He was full of deceit and mischief. The ruins of the old house are in evidence still in the overgrown shrubbery. All traces of a narrow road leading down to the sea and into a cave by way of a secret tunnel have now vanished. The local people feared him because of his loyal henchmen. To them he gave the best holdings in the estate. They responded to his every whim and acted as his private police force and bodyguard, also conspiring with him to enforce his most illegal and vicious behaviour on the common people. His major preoccupation was coveting young maidens of marriageable age, especially females who were about to marry. Their parents were under threat of eviction if the young maiden refused to come at his invitation. She was taken forcibly to live at the Big House until he tired of her companionship. Many beautiful girls were deflowered in this manner and many a babe was born with crooked eyes.'

'Sean, please! I do not want to hear any more, I detest that awful barbarity. It is an evil tale. I can't listen to the depravity and brutality of conduct such as you relate.'

'Moll, please understand. I take no satisfaction from the telling. You are a mature woman, but if the story offends your very nature, then I will cease telling it. Personally, I must tell you I do not separate normal sexual behaviour from love and marriage.'

'Well, Sean, it is only a fleeting revulsion of mine, please continue. I am becoming more and more inquisitive as regards the rest of the story.'

'Your womanly imagination is to be disappointed if you are waiting for the spicy bits,' said Sean. 'Moll, you give me the impression that you are about to enter the convent again and at the same time hiding behind a thin veil of pretended innocence. Moll, will I tell you what I think of you?'

'Oh, please do, Sean.'

'Well I think you are a most beautiful young woman and, God forgive me, I would not like you to enter the convent, at least until you go to bed with me.'

'Sean Moore, give over your blathering gobbledegook and get on with the story and I promise no further interruption,' said Moll.

'The story relates that a very beautiful young woman of the O'Leary clan was taken forcibly to the Big House and ere she departed from her tearful parents, she told them not to be sorrowful, that God would protect her and if all other things failed she would destroy herself on Crooked Eyes. Nessa O'Leary had hidden the berries of the deadly hemlock in her gown. On the other hand, Nessa was born with a very special gift. She commanded a certain hypnotic influence over animals. They actually became docile in her presence. Even the little birds were tame. She was often engaged to train headstrong horses. Some said she had the gift of Saint Francis. The day she was taken, Crooked Eyes had prepared a warm welcome for her. He was a most gracious host and went to every extreme to make her feel at home. He showed her a special bedroom with all the trappings of luxury. He told her not to be afraid, that he would come to see if she was comfortable later that night, hinting that he expected she would receive him with warmth and love. Nessa felt an icy shiver run through her entire body – call it what you will, divine intervention or fate or whatever. His next question to Nessa was to decide his fate, in a simple but tragic manner.

' "Nessa, is it true that you possess a very special gift, that of influence over wild animals?"

' "Yes. This is true, sir," replied Nessa. "I have tamed wild horses by touching them."

'Crooked Eyes shrieked and shook with laughter.

' "Well, Nessa, before this day is over I will put your powers to the test. I brought a bull from Spain to improve my herd, but the Spaniard fooled me. He sold me a bull from the arena. We have tried every trick to tame the beast but he has a legion of devils in him. He will let no man near him."

' "What do you wish me to do with the bull?" said Nessa.

' "If you can, put a blindfold across his eyes. It is a special headgear for wild bulls," said Crooked Eyes.

' "Will you take me to see the animal this evening, if you please? It may take me a while to become friendly with him. I should like to go to his yard immediately or wherever he is kept," said Nessa.

' "Ho, ho," said Crooked Eyes. "You would make a fortune in Spain. What a brave girl you are! I will give you a rapier with which to defend yourself, also a bodyguard consisting of four of my best men, including myself."

' "I will not need any weapon of defence. All I ask is that you or your men do not show yourselves until I have my job done, but keep near at hand. Please give me the head harness and I shall make a start," said Nessa.

'The enclosure where the bull was kept was some distance from the Big House. It had high walls and a narrow entrance with an iron-barred gate. Nessa stood still outside the bars. The great beast turned, as he observed her, with lowered head and needle-pointed horns. He trotted up to the gate, standing like a show-man and swaying his head from side to side, scraping up fragments of mud with his front hooves and casting it on his back. He stood for a while snorting and puffing as if playing to the gallery, then turning suddenly threw his hind hooves high in the air and ran in short circles. Once more he approached where Nessa stood, but this time he was much closer, his front legs spread apart. Nessa put her hands through the bars, only to be met with a snort and a prancing dance, before withdrawing again to a safe distance.

'Nessa spoke in soft whispers to the beast, with her hand outstretched. The creature suddenly came closer and became much less aggressive. He sniffed at Nessa and proceeded to lick her hand. Nessa noticed that three great sliding bolts needed to be unfastened from the head harness. She undid two bolts with her free hand. Crooked Eyes and his men were in waiting only a few yards away, hidden from view. Nessa called them to come to her and not to be afraid: "The bull is now quiet and will not harm you."

'As they came into view, Nessa pulled the last bolt, flinging the gate wide open, and as she did so the captive bull rushed headlong towards the men who fled in all directions. Crooked Eyes ran to gain the safety of the Big House, but the bull was gaining ground and cutting off his escape. Seeing this he turned sharply and ran towards the entrance to the secret tunnel, which was on the pathway that led to the sea. A large lintel of stone was placed over the low narrow opening that supported the cliff face overhead. To gain entrance, a person must turn side first and crawl through. Crooked Eyes reached the opening with the great bull fast on his heels. With only seconds to spare he managed to squeeze through and, crouching within the narrow recess, he taunted the bull, calling: "Toro! Toro! Toro! Warra! Warra! Warra!

Warra!" in deep nasal imitation of a bull, at the same time infuriating the animal by making lunges with the rapier at its nose. The bull, making a violent charge, got its head and massive shoulders stuck beneath the lintel that supported some stone masonry, and in the struggle to extract itself, brought several tons of heavy masonry crashing downwards with the dislodged lintel.

'Nor did it stop at that. A portion of loose, overhanging cliff followed, completely burying the animal and its master within the tunnel. Neighbours, including Nessa's parents, came from far and near and viewed the scene in silence. Two days later they uncovered the body of the dead bull and they extricated the body of semi-conscious Crooked Eyes trapped in the rubble of the entrance. He had suffered multiple injuries and despite the best medical attention he expired after three days. Local folklore mentions the roaring of a wild bull being heard on the hour of his departure from this world. Folk were very superstitious in that age, so let us assume that God, who is love, invited old Crooked Eyes, warts and all, into his heavenly kingdom.

'The Big House fell into decay. The men who had been faithful to him were set upon by the oppressed. The servants fled and eventually the place was burned down. Nessa O'Leary became the bride of Patrick Molloy, your great grandfather. Some years after, during a great storm, the western cheek of the mountain slipped downwards covering our land, which extended in that direction as if wanting to obliterate the memory of that period. Some say his gold is down there still. I hope to find it some day. So, Moll of the raven tresses, I wonder have you inherited any traits of your great ancestors who were high kings of Ireland?'

'Oh no! Sean Moore, that gold is dirty. Do not wish

for it. Gold to become clean must first be washed in poverty. It must be used to help the poor.'

'That is my story, Moll, as I heard it.'

'Thank you, Sean. It is a strange and tragic tale, perhaps part sound and part broken. Sean, it is getting late. Tim is up there in that great mass of rock for two hours or more. Come, let us go to find him.'

'Moll, don't worry! Your brother has all his back teeth. I have something more important to discuss with you. In fact I do not know how to say it. It concerns a woman, so please bear with me.'

'A woman, Sean! What woman? Who is she? Out with it. Why have you not told me of a woman in your life before now?'

'Easy, Moll, easy! Come back to ground. I asked you to listen.'

'Yes, Sean, tell me about this woman.'

'Now, Moll, this woman is none other than yourself. I have admired you for years, so this is my question: Will you be my wife? I will not press you for an answer and I hope I have not caused you distress.'

Moll was sitting beside Sean. She glanced at him with a startled look, then in a little ripple of smothered laughter, placed her head between cupped palms and stayed in this position for some moments until Sean spoke again: 'It is all right Moll, don't let it upset you.' When she lifted her head, her usual marble pallor had disappeared and the cheeks of the dark maiden were tinged with a red blush. 'Come, Sean Moore,' she said. 'Let us find our Tim, but before we go I will give you my answer.'

Placing her arms around his neck, she laid her lips to his in a long lingering overflow of built-up, secret desire for the man whom she liked most. They walked together in silence to the Claddarach. There now existed a mutual understanding between them. All the barriers and barricades were uprooted and replaced with a trust that was sealed with a kiss. Shades of evening were already falling on the Claddarach; the chill of winter in the air, the dark grey slate cliffs devoid of vegetation and the shadows of moving clouds cast a grotesque, ghostly imagery on the strewn slabs and boulders. Moll was first to break the silence:

'This place gives me the creeps! I feel as if the place is haunted. Up here somewhere old Crooked Eyes met his doom. I wish I had never listened to that tale. Tim is nowhere to be seen. Something dreadful has befallen him.'

'Take it easy, Moll. He will come back. Let's call him.'

'Yes Sean. I will give the whistle signal we use when calling each other on the island.'

Moll placed her little finger to form an arc across her lower lip and produced a long piercing whistle. Moving forward towards the towering cliffs, Moll repeated the whistle at intervals. Then came a faint reply from behind. They retraced their footsteps in the direction from where it was heard. They were receiving a stronger signal, which was much nearer the house. Then came a cry: 'Over here!' Scrambling across the broken rock face as quickly as possible in the direction of the call, they found him lying on the ground, utterly exhausted. Moll knelt beside him while Sean tried to lift his prone body. Moll shook with suppressed laughter. He was a sight to behold. His jacket, or what remained of it, was in tatters. One sleeve was entirely missing.

'He must have crawled a long distance on his hands and knees,' said Sean. 'He has also lost his tweed cap.'

'Can you walk, Tim?' said Moll.

'No, Moll! No! I want to lie here and die. Thank

God you found me. It is a dreadful place, full of chimney soot and every sort of rubbish.'

'Ah,' said Sean. 'It is a souterrain. The little men who built these underground chambers were the Fir Bolgs. They went underground and lived in them, for some reason or other.'

'Wild cats are down there!' said Tim. 'They hissed and spat at me and stared with their green eyes. One long, sleekly creature slid by in the muddy ooze.'

'That was a water dog,' said Sean. 'The Claddarach is a playground for otters.'

'Let's not delay talking, before we all die of cold,' said Moll.

'How are we to take him?' said Sean. 'I will go back to the house for a wheelbarrow.'

'Ah, a wheelbarrow, your bottom,' said Moll. 'A giant like you, and my brother not as heavy as a slung calf!'

'But just as filthy,' said Sean.

'Throw him across your shoulders, or he will die where he lies,' said Moll.

Bending down with the minimum of effort, Sean Moore swung Tim's half-limp body over his shoulder. The house was only a short distance away. On entering the kitchen they laid him near the warmth of the open hearth. Moll reverted to uncontrolled laughter.

Tim said feebly: 'Moll, why do you make so light of my condition?'

'Because you remind me of Topsy, in *Uncle Tom's Cabin*,' said Moll.

'Yes!' retorted Tim. 'Topsy was black, but her soul was white, whiter than yours.'

Moll did not answer, but prepared a hot drink for her brother. Sean half-filled a great wooden tub with warm water in the back kitchen, where he helped Moll with bathing, scrubbing and rubbing Tim, despite his protestations, until his skin glowed with a crimson blush and the wine of life flowed normally through the rivers of his flesh once more. They fixed a bed in Sean's room and wrapped him in warm blankets and gave him warm nourishing food. It was then he told them how when he searched for the secret tunnel, suddenly a thin slab broke beneath his feet, causing him to fall into an underground bunker. With great effort he crawled along a narrow fissure, led by a flicker of light from above that brought him to safety. Tim complained of pain in his hip joint, but Sean assured him that it was only bruised, after asking him to do a few simple exercises. 'You may have to use crutches for a couple of weeks, but the doctor will decide that,' said Sean.

Sean and Moll prepared a meal, which they enjoyed, having washed all trace of soot from their persons.

'You will have to take it easy now, Tim, and don't dare leave your bed,' said Moll. 'Sean and I will go across to the island. I need to bring some clothes for you and also some bed clothing. What you were wearing is not fit for the ragman. Your old injury is worse and we must stay until you are well able to travel. You are to do as I say, Tim.'

'I promise that, Moll,' said Tim.

It was a wonderful night, such as is seldom seen in winter. The wheel of the great silver disc wore a sheen of scintillating brilliance, and was bathed in a soft green-grey light. The only clouds to be seen were a few white puffballs resting without movement on the far horizon. The lights of a passing ship moving steadily on course served to betray the presence of man. Surely a night for lovers, a night to be alone with nature, a night to look into the beauty of the unknown, a night for man to pose a simple question! Why was the sand so soft and silvery underfoot? Moll was first to speak: 'Sean, you seem to be moonstruck! Why are you so silent, all the time gazing into space? Maybe you were born in the full of the moon and the full of the tide. In other words, one half an *amadán*!'

Snatching his cap, she ran swiftly by him in the soft dry sand. Sean gained ground and quickly brought her on to the sand in a gentle tackle. She rolled over on her back, while he pinned both her outstretched arms in the form of a cross. Yes! As she lay there unresisting there was a wild beautiful light in her eyes. Sean released her hands and rolled over on his back beside her.

'Sean,' said Moll, 'are you not going to return that kiss I gave you this evening?'

'You just want your kiss back,' said Sean. 'I had thought you gave me that kiss to keep forever.'

Moll jumped to her feet, exclaiming: 'Then keep it forever. I will not marry you, Sean Moore!'

Moll, despite her show of spiritedness, was too slow for Sean, who seized her around the ankles and brought her to the ground in a flurry of sand. She suddenly became strangely passive. When she spoke again she said: 'Sean, we are behaving like little children. Let us go across to the island.'

'Not before I return your kiss,' said Sean.

A little cloud like a curtain drew across the face of the moon and a little sand chick running by the beach seemed to utter: 'Tut! Tut! Tut!'

> In monomania I can find,
> One damsel to my mind,
> Two in Leinster,
> And in England, many.

But if I had my choice,
How much would I rejoice,
To wed thee,
Dark maiden of the valley!

THE RED PETTICOAT

Many years have passed since I saw a woman dressed in a red petticoat. The following story wells into mind concerning some friends of mine and the girl in the red petticoat. My friends, more fortunate than I, were sent to secondary schools. Jack qualified as a schoolteacher, Joe became an inspector of schools and Jim got a job with the Gaelic Department. One day while on summer holidays we decided to cycle around the Ring of Kerry. Only gentlemen students owned bicycles in those days. Although not a student, a bicycle was provided for me for the journey.

Starting out from Ballinskelligs in the early morning we found ourselves passing by a place called Ballybog, somewhere between Sneem and Kenmare. The time being about one o'clock, we decided to break our journey and rest for a while. While we chatted we admired the beautiful countryside and the people working in the bogs nearby. One young woman in particular who worked alone attracted our attention. She was wearing a bright red petticoat.

Joe ventured: 'I'll bet she was never kissed in her life! One thing I know, she was never kissed by you and she never will be!'

'Don't be so sure,' said Jack. 'I might take you up on that.'

'I'll bet you half a crown,' said Joe.

'You haven't the courage to go in there yourself and ask her for a kiss,' said Jack. 'Make it three half-crowns then and you're on.'

'I can't afford seven shillings and sixpence,' said Joe.

It was at this juncture that Jim and myself put up the required money, half a crown each. Seven shillings and sixpence was a fortune then. Now I must let Jack tell the story:

'Leaving my bicycle by the side of the road I set off across the bogland which was about a quarter of a mile distant. Their last advice was: "You must at least try to kiss her, Jack. How do you feel? Don't get cold feet!" I did not deign to answer them. I had to present a defiant front to my tormentors. In all honesty, I was not feeling very confident about how I would approach the matter. Walking slowly, I picked bunches of bog cotton. I drew near to the peat bank where the young woman worked stacking the sods into little heaps to be wind-dried. She had not yet noticed my coming and was in a stooped position and barefooted. Her collops in contrast with her red petticoat were white as snow, her hair a raven black. I must not alarm her, I thought. I could hear her humming the air of a song that I knew well, "An Cailín Deas Crúite na mBó" or "The Pretty Maid Milking her Cow".

'What excuse would I come up with? Would I tell her who I was? Too late! She turned and faced me. Already I could see hostility in her eyes, eyes as dark as a thunderstorm over the Black Valley. "Good evening," I ventured, "you are working hard." She did not reply. "My name is Jack Sullivan from Ballinskelligs. I am cycling to Killarney with my pals. Could you kindly tell me some place that would serve tea and sandwiches?"

'I must have struck the wrong chord, as she completely ignored my question, and why not? What a place to enquire about a tea house, in the middle of a south Kerry bog, after just passing through a village with a tavern and an eating house! Feeling very stupid, I said: "It's a long time since I footed turf," as I moved a little closer to her. Bending down, I made heaps of the turf into neat little stands of about a dozen sods. All to no avail. Like the elusive wagtail, she always kept at a safe distance, a wild Irish rose, unbridled, unsaddled, unkissed and untamed. Since "music hath charms", I tried my last ruse, saying: "I will sing you a song before I go. You were humming 'The Pretty Maid Milking her Cow' just as I came. It is my favourite song."

> Had I the wealth of great Omar.
> Or all on the African shore,
> Or had I great Devonshire's treasure
> Or had I ten thousand times more,
> Or had I the lamp of Aladdin,
> And had I his genius also,
> I'd rather live poor on a mountain
> With *Cailín Deas Crúite na mBó*.

'Then she surprised me by singing the next verse. What an enthralling voice! Moving closer, she held me spellbound. Her voice floated ethereal on the airy, summer-soft zephyr.

> I beg you withdraw and don't tease me
> I cannot consent unto thee
> I prefer to live single and airy,
> Till more of the world I see.
> New cares they would me embarrass,

Beside, sir, my fortune is low,
Until I get rich I'll not marry!
Said the pretty maid milking her cow.

'Turning to her I said: "I must leave now. I hope we will meet again. Your voice is heavenly. Can I kiss you for that?"

' "Indeed you will not!" she said with a frightened look in her eyes. "I will call my brothers who are working in the bog over there."

'It was then I pounced and placed a kiss somewhere on her beautiful face. Emitting a piercing shriek like a banshee, the Amazonian goddess tore free from my embrace. Stooping low she grabbed a coal-black brick of hard peat, which she bounced off my left cheekbone with deadly accuracy, making me see stars and starting rivers of claret to run. Then I saw men from other bogs come running towards us. Deciding that a good run is better than a bad stand, with blood streaming down my side face I ran and waved her goodbye. I saw her shudder and cover her eyes with her apron. Maybe I broke some records for bog trotting, but I outstripped my pursuers who eventually turned their attention to the young woman with the red petticoat.

'When I reached the roadside my pals were very concerned, seeing the wound on my cheekbone.

' "What really happened?" they said. "We saw you embrace her."

' "What really happened is I won my wager, so hand over those three half crowns!"

'Which they promptly did. Then I said: "I will bet ten shillings for one or all three of you to go over and do the same."

'All three having declined, I called them by names

known to hard-case skippers or captains of pirate ships. I used vitriolic, abrasive and sulphuric words before mounting my bicycle and continuing with my lily-livered companions to Killarney.'

Our First Forbidden Tryst

The old boreen was sultry.
Berry-bunched briars
Climbed the furze
Ripe with black blood.
In the next field
Speckled cows
Lay lazily, cud bursting,
Drinking lungfuls
Of haw-scented air.
What harm if we trampled
Long-dried, crispy cow-turd!
The night was silver.

I was stepping seventeen,
My breasts were taut;
Within, a clasp of fire.
John gazed moonward
With starry, fear-filled eyes.
Was it the innocence
Of our first forbidden tryst?
Moonbeams played pranks.
Soft shafts were on my hair
And on his face.
He was beautiful.
I pouted rounded kisses
Mixed with smiles
Each time he looked,
And touched his moon-silvered cheek.

Hush! We heard the old priest
Walking alone
On the back road,
A wooden tapping of the blackthorn
On the gravel
Like a warning bell.

Enjoy the silver of the night!
Darkness is only for the groping.
Great sighs of satisfaction burst
From mound-bellied, sprawling cows.
The boreen was warm,
Warm with the incense
Of bleeding blackberries.
The old priest passed on.

Coinne

Do Bhrian Ó Dochartaigh

The previous poem, 'Our First Forbidden Tryst', is a free translation of this poem, first published in the collection Barra Taoide *in 1988.*

Bhí an bóithrín
meirbh le coinne
agus mise corraithe
ag feitheamh,
mo chíocha
teann le tine
i nglasnasc an ghrá.
Cén díobháil satailt
ar bhualtacha feoite
cearcaillí féarghlas
ag borradh uathu!
Ba breaca
taobh thall de chlaí
ina luí,
ag scéith
le huachtar buí,
Ag brúchtaíl
is ag osnaíl,
ag cogaint a gcíorach
is ag casadh na ngar.
Bhí drisleoga
ina crotháin chraobhaing
crochta ar ghuaille,
an t-aiteann bláfar

go caor bheirteach sméarach
nuair a d'éalaigh sé
im dháil.

Sheas sé suas
taobh liom
ag féachaint
le hionadh
ar phíosa geal airgid
lánroth na ré;
in ionad na réalt
ag spréacharnaigh
ina shúile
bhí faitíos an neamhchiontais –
b'fhéidir eagla roimh mhná.
B'é seo ár gcéad choinne
fé cheilt
fé chosc
fé thoirmeasc
i ngáirdín an tsóigh.

Bhí gathaí ré ag cleasaíocht
is ag caitheamh
saigheada boga linn.
Chum mé ciorcal le mo bheola
chun é a phógadh.
D'fhéach sé orm
go fonnmhar;
Roinneas bláthfhleasc,
gathaí gléineach,
ar a éadan
le mo mhéara.

Huis, éist
leis an sagart críonna
ag siúl ina aonar
ar an mbóthar iata,
buillí beaga
maide draighne
mar chloigín adhmaid
ag tomhas na hoíche.
Bainig taitneamh
as an solas
is leis an útamálaí an dorchadas.
Osnaíl ba breaca
lán sochma
'na luí,
brúchtaíl anála
le clos thar claí,
bóithrín meirbh
le túis chumhra
agus sú dearg
ó sméara dubha.

Cloigín adhmaid
ina thost cois falla,
sagart críonna
síoch ina chodladh.

COURTING COUPLES AND THE PARISH PRIEST

Company-keeping between boys and girls was frowned upon by the Church. It was seen as the prelude to pre-marital, illicit sexual relations. People mentioned it in several different ways. It was referred to as 'courting', 'dyking', 'mousing', 'clicking' and 'whistling'. In other languages they had their own set of names for the oldest game on earth, and in Gaelic it was given a host of names also, including the 'game of the sod' or 'grassy sward'.

I heard many spine-chilling sermons shouted angrily from the pulpit, warning us that we were walking on the brink of the fiery abyss of Hell in secret company-keeping, together with the evil of the dancing hall and the dark ways home.

Maybe it is well that we ponder on the concern of the Church at that period, of the good priests who tried to shield us from the effects of our own ignorance and also from the powerful pull of our humanity, natural desire and craving for sensual gratification. But the question remains – Why the ignorance?

The old parish priest who sallied forth in the dark of the night or maybe in the full of the moon, brandishing a stout thorn stick, was known to patrol the highways and byways, routing and scattering illicit lovers from their trysting places. The holy man was only the good shepherd, tending his wayward flock as his bounden duty – or so he regarded it. Of course this was considered a very serious business but it was not without its funny side.

I remember one young blade who decided with the help of others to dress as a bogus priest. Complete with black clothing, white collar and broad black felt hat, he looked the real thing. On his first foray among the erring Christians, he caused consternation among a group of crossroad dancers who scattered in all directions. All was well until he met up with the real parish priest who was hunting courting couples on the same night. The parish priest addressed the bogus priest: 'Goodnight, Father!' The bogus padre took a flying leap over the roadside fence, disappearing into the darkness in an instant. Not a word was said about the matter for many a long day. Some say the old padre did not appear on the road again.

A Bridal Morning

For Nancy and Max

I remember
Wearing
A shimmering
Silken gown
When summer sun
Peeped gently
From the hill,
And, like a molten apple,
Spilled milk of gold
Across my window sill,
Which overflowed
Into the boudoir
Of my soul,
And lit shy blushes
In a garden
Ripe with leaf,
Where blossoms
Of the May
Hung scented deep.

Now I search
The arbour of my heart,
Alas, to ask
Why did it fade
Into the past?
Why did the north winds
Sing so harsh,
Searing the petals

A Bridal Morning

From the garland
Of my crown?
And why did
The rains come down?

HASTE TO THE WEDDING

A far cry from the lavishness, flair and showy extravagance of today were the Shrovetide weddings of my youth. When my relative Tom Fenton from Coom married Margaret McCarthy from the Glen, the wedding was to remain indelible in my memory, I being only seven years and some months. That morning I was given in care to the local postman, who would pass by the wedding house on his daily delivery. This extra duty, on the instructions of my mother, was to escort me to and leave me safely at the Fenton dwelling. My mother would follow later and help other women to prepare the wedding feast.

Ned Walsh was the postman's name and a more kind and loving person you could not wish for. He made my journey comfortable and exciting by sitting me astride the saddle of the first bicycle I can remember seeing in the locality. Rural postmen were not supplied with any means of transport and mail was delivered on foot. How Ned came by the bicycle I do not know, as bicycles were a very scarce commodity for years to come. The road to Coom was of rough, loose stone called gravel and was very steep, but we arrived safely at my cousin's house. Ned was invited to the wedding, being an able performer on the melodeon. He could play all night long set tunes, jigs, reels, hornpipes and old-time waltzes. Later in life, I heard him play such tunes as 'Haste to the Wedding', 'Bean ag Baint Duileasc' ('The

Woman Cutting Dulse'), 'You Broke my Cups and
Saucers', 'Garden of Daisies', 'Boney's Retreat' and others, too numerous to mention here.

On reaching the Fenton farmhouse I saw many
women neighbours preparing the wedding feast. I was
very relieved to see my mother arriving and working
with them later on. Some were busy tending to great
black iron pots. One contained rich savoury beef broth,
hanging on the swing crane within the chimney breast.
Another pot was full of flowery potatoes, bursting their
jackets. Several kitchen tables lent by neighbours for the
feast were placed end to end. Ned was given a
tomhaisín (a little measure) of whiskey and also a big
dark glass of porter with a white collar of rich, creamy
foam. We were both seated to table, each with a generous supply of corned beef and cabbage and a plentiful
amount of delicious beef broth and potatoes. Ned
noticed that I seemed very shy. He would occasionally
whisper and say: 'Don't be shy! Eat up, boy, or you'll
never grow up if you don't eat up!' When all the tables
were set, fancy tablecloths were not displayed, but all
tables scrubbed white and laden with great portions of
roast goose and mutton on beautiful patterned earthenware plates. There was a choice of good, wholesome
food, from home-cured bacon and cabbage to the entire
pig's head, complete with snout and ears scraped clean.

All was ready for the wedding party, which would
soon arrive, after celebrating at Paddy Keating's or at
Haren's licensed premises in Ballinskelligs. Another
spare table was heaped with several loaves of homemade bread, some known as curranty cakes and baked
several days previously, in the round oven on the
hearthstone covered with live coals. Also a plentiful
supply of baker's bread called *builíní bána*, white loaves

dubbed by us country folk as 'shop bread'. There was plenty of red jam in earthenware crocks and china jugs and a supply of homemade fresh butter.

The wedding party could now be seen appearing around the road leading into Coom. This bend is known by the Gaelic word, *an Lúb* (the bend). I remember seeing several jaunting cars and farm carts coming into view, also single riders on saddle horses. The strains of sweet music from a melodeon drifted upwards along the valley from the homeward cavalcade, giving the evening a joyful air of festivity. The kitchen soon filled with guests, who were mostly small farmers, their wives, a few fishermen and a good few young boys and girls. A special table was set up in the centre for the bride and groom. The bride wore a long skirt of heavy blue material, the hem of which helped sweep the floor. Her footwear was not totally visible, except for little glimpses of soft, polished black leather. Margaret was a very handsome woman who had spent some time in America. She was dressed in a white blouse with a very high collar reaching under her chin, sleeves that were long, wide and full, covering the wrists and the back of her hands, and a bright brooch with brilliant, flashing eyes adorning the front of her neck. All flesh was left to the imagination of the beholder, in contrast to the modern creations of our present fashion, making brides and mothers of that era look like packages labelled 'not to be opened till Christmas'. The bride's coiffure was her crowning glory. Her fair auburn hair was coiled into plaited rings turban-like on the back slope of her head, supported by ornate combs with sparkling coloured eyes, which were beads of glass. Looking back now, I think the dress had a genteel suggestion of Victorianism.

When the meal was finished the tables were stowed to

make room for dancing, singing and drinking; also perhaps some furtive courtship. Two wooden casks of stout, with very thick oak staves, stood on a table in the back porch, attended by a special, trustworthy person, a neighbour or close relative of the family. The drink was distributed in pint-glass measures and care taken that some were not favoured more than others. It was well known that a bucketful of stout could disappear mysteriously into the night to regale a stag party held secretly behind the barn or a haystack in the haggard. Therefore the person in charge had to be vigilant, lest any fast ones were pulled. In latter years I heard drinkers praise the viscosity of the black beverage of those days, saying: 'Sure there was eating and drinking in it!', 'Wouldn't the glass stick to the counter!' and 'It was like black honey compared to what we're drinking now, pure bog water [*uisce na gcos*], and look at the price of it!'

The young unmarried women wore their hair long and plaited, but were dressed much the same as the older women. All wore black woollen shawls. A few yellow or brown shawls were in vogue later on. Some young girls were wearing white blouses. Fashion was changing from 1912 onwards.

The dance commenced with old-time sets and four-hand reels. Nano Roche, the groom's mother, took off her leather shoes and danced a superb Irish reel in her vamps. The hearth flagstone had a hollow sound. Some said it was laid across an empty iron pot in order to give a staccato effect to the tap dancing. Paddy Lawlor, whom I knew in later life, was a young man then. He danced 'The Sailor's Hornpipe'. Others danced jigs, making a merry drumming sound of hollow reverberations. All footwear was fashioned by local shoemakers, who vied with each other as to who won the most customers. Men's footwear, whether light or heavy, had in most cases iron-tipped heels. Some women wore buckled shoes.

Invariably the petticoat was woollen and the colour very often was a bright red of finely woven flannel. The woman with the red petticoat complete with apron was a common sight during my growing years. As the night wore on, songs were sung. An old man would take the singer's hand in his, rocking the arm to and fro in rhythm with the air of the song. This was called *sean nós* (old style). My brother Paddy sang a song called 'The Shamrock Shore'.

> In the blooming spring when the small birds sing,
> And lambs did sport and play,
> My way I took and friends forsook,
> Till I came to Dublin Quay,
> I entered on board as a passenger,
> To England I sailed o'er.
> I bid farewell to all my friends,
> Round the dear old Shamrock Shore.

Another beautiful song was sung in Gaelic by Maurice Fenton, 'An Buachaill Caol Dubh', about a maiden lamenting the loss of her 'Slender Dark Boy'. John Fitzgerald from Horse Island sang a very old English song, which I heard many times in later life, and which has never lost its charm, called 'After the Ball Was Over'. Annie Fenton from Caherdaniel sang a very old song called 'Lucky Jim', and 'Siúl, A Rún'.

> I would I were on yonder hill,
> 'Tis there I'd sit and cry my fill,
> And every tear would turn a mill,
> *Is go dté tú, mo mhuirnín, slán.*
> I'll dye my petticoats, I'll dye them red,

And round the world I'll beg my bread,
Until my parents shall wish me dead,
Is go dté tú, mo mhuirnín, slán.

Weddings are an occasion of rejoicing and happiness
but there is always the danger of arguments if Bacchus
is allowed to influence rational thinking. In this case
two neighbours got involved in a silly argument relating
to the best method of castrating calves and piglets,
which was practised by lay people. One accused the
other jocosely of bringing home the testicles and grilling
them on the fire tongs as tasty morsels. The jocose word
spoken without malice can often contain the germ of
offence, which can perchance lead to fiery emotion. In
this case, a free-for-all was avoided by the intervention
of their good spouses, who prevailed on their bellicose
husbands to shake hands and have a little common
sense, thus avoiding an outbreak of hostilities among
good neighbours.

The feasting continued until early dawn. Food was
again prepared for all the guests, who were called to the
table in turn. A table in the parlour had several brass
candlesticks with wax candles lighting. I remember
drooping slowly to sleep in a soft chair beside my
mother. All I can recall is that my eyes faltered, and I
was seeing beautiful coloured rainbows of light encircling each candle flame. The miracle of suspended consciousness being so deep, I was surprised to wake in my
own bed in Ballinskelligs, late next day. How I arrived
there is only known to my good and caring mother who
moulded my growing years!

As I grew in age I was present at other weddings,
which followed much the same pattern. Local boys would
dress in costumes consisting of funny tunics and hats

made entirely from sheaves of oaten straw. A group of those young boys and girls visited the wedding house without invitation. They were always treated with tolerance and courtesy, given refreshments and allowed to dance with the bride. They also carried their own musical instruments. This was an old traditional custom in most parish communities, to go 'strawing'.

A story is told of a girl who was forced into a marriage of loveless convenience by her parents. On her wedding night, when festivities were at their height, her lover came disguised as a straw-boy, complete in his costume and mask. During the dance with the bride, who recognized him as her former sweetheart, she whispered: 'Please come for me before dawn breaks and bring your horse.' The story tells how the horse was found cropping grass peacefully on the roadside somewhere near Cork city. A farewell note with the following poem and a straw-boy's hat were found attached to the bridle:

America lies far away,
A place we soon will be.
Let those be damned forever,
Who would part my love from me.

People who could not provide transport were satisfied to walk to church and home again, to partake of whatever fare they were able to afford. They raised fine families, living good Christian lives and were mostly contented with their lot. Some weddings were frowned upon by one or both sets of parents. It is said that 'marriages are made in heaven', but I venture to say a number of very doubtful ones are made on earth. That a marriage should be valid it was most important that the mutual consent of the contracting parties was fully

observed. Eloping couples were very few. Only a coura-
geous girl would throw a bundle of her wearing apparel
into the night, and follow by wriggling out through a
narrow gable window and down a short ladder provided
for her, into the waiting arms of her swain. Perhaps the
next letter received by her distraught parents would
come from lovers on their way to the New World. However, marriage was not always by the mutual consent of
the contracting parties. Some couples were forced into
marriage by domineering parents and clergy, who would
not tolerate a hint of pregnancy, let alone illegitimacy in
their families. The edict pertaining to such a transgres-
sion was marry or abscond, or else risk becoming a
social pariah among the self-righteous parish Pharisees.

> The night of the wedding,
> The night of the fun,
> The night of the wedding,
> She had a young son.

Young women were usually left holding the burden
of blame and so-called shame. They became the sacrifi-
cial lambs on the altar of a slowly emerging, modern,
democratic, partly Christian society. Many never
entered the marriage bed but cursed the day they were
joined in dubious wedlock. Who has not heard of the
shotgun wedding!

A story is told of a young man who denied being
responsible for a young girl with whom he was friendly,
but who now appeared to be pregnant. In good faith
their parents and the local parish priest used their good
influence to persuade the couple to marry. The match-
makers considered that the pair should do the decent
thing and thereby avoid a scandal. When all seemed
serene on the nuptial morning, as the bride approached

the church accompanied by her parents, she was seen to suddenly swoon and fall to the ground. The priest was immediately summoned to her side, and he in turn ordered medical attention. The doctor performed an on-the-spot diagnosis, declaring that the girl was not pregnant and in his opinion she had nothing more exciting inside her at that moment than an excessive amount of superfluous gas trapped within her intestines. So ended what otherwise could be termed a mild case of shotgun pressure, much to the relief of the proud parents.

At my uncle's wedding, a local woman named Kate was detailed to attend to the milking of the cows that evening. Night had fallen at six o'clock and it was dark in the byre where the cows were tied in their stalls. Six cows were in one byre and in another smaller house were tied two cows and a mule. I was to accompany her with extra buckets and a lantern – a rough type of carriage lamp with a candle and glass sides. All went well while she milked the six cows. We took the pails of milk to the dairy and strained it through a muslin cloth into the tubs where it accumulated for churning. In the dairy standing on a small table was a barrel of stout, with a tap and a white enamel bucket ready with several pint measures to treat the guests when the wedding party arrived. Each time we visited the dairy Kate would fill herself a pint glass of porter. I know she drank it with gusto because of the smacking sounds she made with her lips and a satisfied exhalation of her breathing ending in an 'Ah! Ah!' of relish. She offered me some to drink. When I declined she said it was good for me.

Lastly we entered the small byre where the other two cows and the mule were in their stalls. On handing her the little milking stool, it was at this juncture that some sudden gust of air puffed out the candle flame within the lantern, leaving us in complete darkness. I groped and fumbled with the matchbox, in a hurry to strike a light. In the meantime I heard Kate chuckle to herself, saying: 'Hurry boy, light the candle quick. There is something strange here. I think this cow has a pair of balls.' I heard her shout of laughter as I got the lantern going. She had mistaken the mule for a cow in the darkness. Kate was a jolly, warm-hearted person, very good-humoured and loved a joke.

A few summers ago I was a guest at a wedding with much of the modern trappings. The dinner and reception were held at a special venue. In contrast with the old-style country weddings, for me it was a repetitious, uninteresting and boring affair. We listened to impromptu speeches extolling the qualities of one or other of the newlyweds, punctuated with intervals of readings from telegrams, cards, etc. The hired band played blaring, ear-splitting disco music, making ordinary conversation barely audible. The antics on the dance floor seemed not so much good physical exercise as a carbon copy of some ritual dance performed at a tribal feast in Africa. Gone were the old-time jigs, reels and Irish dancing.

A Living Salmon

A foolish fisherman,
I diced with love,
And cast my lure
With good intent.
I did present
To her
A living, silver salmon.

I did not weigh
My foolish whim
Within the silver scales
That blind the eyes
Of those who trust.
They see no guile
Awaiting
In the grass.

Alas, to see
The greedy poacher
Without an oar,
A sail or boat,
Come striding
Down the street
And neatly tucked
In his linked arm
My living silver salmon.

STATIONS OF LIFE

Paddy Buckley sat by the open kitchen fireplace, gazing thoughtfully into the leaping flame coming from a great peat fire on the hearthstone. It was just one week since he had buried his mother in the Abbey below. Alone in his silence, he pondered over his new situation in life. A free man again, free from obligation or urgent commitments; or so he thought. He was a bachelor and an only son. His father had died tragically when he was yet a *garsún*. His horse had bolted and capsized the cart on the mountain road, pinning his father underneath. Paddy was forty-five years old on his last birthday. He was growing old; he looked up at the old clock with its weights and chains, with its dull metallic tick-tock, mercilessly measuring away his years of youthfulness. Yes, there were questions to be answered. Why did he never marry? Why this? Why that? Why did he waste his years helping his mother run the farm, until she became too feeble for any further work?

But Paddy had no regrets. He had been a good son. He had provided every comfort for his mother in her ailing years. His farmland was excellent and gave him a good return. He could not blame his mother, who had often advised him to bring in a wife. Somehow he had never responded to her entreaties. It was a strange feeling. Now only a week since her funeral, the house seemed so empty, the very heartbeat of life seemed to have departed from the house in her passing. Only yesterday he had been speaking with the parish priest, settling accounts, dealing with Church dues and his mother's death. Ah! He'd get used to being alone. But hadn't the good priest given him advice. 'It is bad for a man to live alone. Look around for a suitable partner,' he had said. Maybe he wasn't too old yet. The best advice of all the priest gave him was to choose some girl who in his opinion might be fruitful – just in case he was tempted to tie-up with some scald-crow, who would nag and comb his hair with the poker for the rest of his life. And, adding another little attachment, the priest proclaimed: 'It would be wise for you now to have the Stations in the house when your turn comes next month.'

Paddy took advantage of the rainy days to prepare for the Stations. First he decided the dresser would need a wash down and a new coat of paint. Removing all the delph, he found an old flat tin box on top of the dresser in a concealed position. As he took it down, he seemed to forget that twenty years had elapsed since he had placed it there. On opening it he found two documents: one was a copy of the title deed to his holding, left by his father. The other was a letter. Both documents had yellowed with age. Paddy recognized the letter, the postmark barely discernible except for the words, 'Mass., USA', the abbreviation of Massachusetts State. He read it once more.

> Dear Pat,
> I am here in the welfare hospital, on the flat of my back, where last week I gave birth to your offspring, a beautiful baby girl. I have called her after myself, Brigid Sullivan. I do not blame you entirely. It was I who gave myself to you, both body and

soul, but you chose to hide it from your mother, afraid of the shame I might bring on your people. I forgive you the pain you caused me, because you suffered from a false un-Christian pride practised by our people.

Brigid is beautiful. She has wonderful dark eyes. At least God and nature intended that she be part of you. I will never abandon her even if she will never know her father. At least I am happy I didn't bring a scandal into your life.

Goodbye,
Brigid.

This was the letter he had put into the box twenty years ago, the letter that bore no address except for the vague postmark. It would remain the skeleton in the cupboard of his memory. Often he had pondered long and deeply about Brigid, the one great love in his life, and the events that to this day haunted him with remorse. Why did he let her emigrate? Why did he listen to the self-righteous hypocrites who laid the foundations for moral behaviour? Why did he keep the letter in the first place, in the same tin box with the title deed of his father's farm? Maybe there was a meaning after all.

The rain spilled in torrents against the window, making the interior of the kitchen a little dark. Suspending work on the dresser, he pulled his chair close to the warm glowing fire. The good priest had said it was bad for a man to be alone, alone with a myriad of thoughts flitting through his mind; gloomy, morbid signals coming from old cells that had registered all when he opened the tin box again. Damn the letter anyway. Why not burn it? Bad for man to live alone ... rubbish. All very well for Father Brown ... marry out of cold blood! Words of an old rhyme sounded true:

If you go to the fair,
To buy a mare.
Choose her well,
Don't buy a kicker!

No doubt Father Brown had a housekeeper, but there was a vast difference between a wife and a housekeeper: What must he do to find a wife? Go to dances? He hadn't entered a dance hall in twenty years. Go to the local pub? He hadn't gone to the local in ages. Spending good money ... spouting small talk about fairs and cattle prices. What young one would want that? What about an ad in the paper? How should he word it?

> Bachelor, single, aged forty, devout RC, good dairy farm. Living alone now, but looked after aging mother until she died. Money in bank. Would like to meet sensible, pleasant girl. (Sweet-tempered, with or without family outside of marriage.)
> PS Very musical and good performer on the accordion. Also good cook.

There ended his reverie. All these nonsensical thoughts he must banish from his mind. He'd have the Stations. As for dances, pubs and advertisements, no. Too late, my love, too late. I'm a free man and free I'll remain, he decided.

Now that he had figured it all out, he'd make his mind easy. It was reading the letter that had triggered it all, together with the hassle of preparing for the Stations. Reaching up to the high shelf over the fireplace he took down the button accordion. He hadn't played for a long time. It was a sweet-toned instrument made by Hohner in Germany. He played some beautiful plaintive airs, closing his eyes, thereby shutting out all external reality. He drank in the lovely, soul-soothing, enchanting notes of Moore's 'The Last Rose of Summer' and 'The Meeting of the Waters'. His mind began to fill with a yearning for his youth, or perhaps an evocation of an early love life. Mingled with his music he could vaguely detect a discordant note coming from somewhere in the kitchen. Ceasing to play, he listened to what was a knocking on the kitchen door. Placing his accordion on the kitchen table, he opened the door. Outside Paddy saw what appeared to be a drenched female standing in the rain. Throwing the door wide-open he cried: 'Please come in out of the rain!'

'I'm so sorry to bother you,' the young woman said. 'I have a problem. My bicycle has a broken wheel and I must go back to Cahersiveen this evening. Where can I get help?'

'First of all, come inside and perhaps I can arrange to help get you to town later,' said Paddy. 'Won't you remove your coat? You must be drenched. Draw near to the fire.'

Paddy presented the woman with a dry towel as she proceeded to remove her jacket. Her hair looked more like tresses of wet seaweed that hung limp from the Gownach Rock at low water than the locks of a sweet young girl.

'It is a dreary day,' ventured Paddy. 'You are a tourist, I presume?'

'Yes.' She answered. 'My mother is with friends in Cahersiveen. We are staying for two weeks in Ireland. We come from Springfield, Massachusetts. I have come to south Kerry on business. I'm anxious to meet a supposed relative of mine from my father's side.'

Now she had dried her hair and felt more comfortable sitting by the warm fire. Paddy asked her if she would like refreshments of any kind. She gladly accepted, saying she would like some tea, if it were not too much trouble. 'I'm a good cook and well used to preparing my own meals,' was the one thing Paddy boasted while he busied himself preparing some toast.

'Where is your wife then?' the woman asked.

'I'm living alone,' said Paddy.

'Oh. I should not have asked,' she said. 'My mother's name is Sullivan. I am to visit the parochial house tomorrow and look up the parish records for information regarding my father's people. I presume Father Brown is the parish priest. Am I anywhere near the presbytery? Maybe I could meet with him this evening?'

'You are nearly there,' said Paddy. 'It's only a short mile from here. And funny you should mention Father Brown. I was speaking with him only yesterday. I am to have what we in Ireland call the Stations, which is a Mass celebrated in some house in the neighbourhood each year. This year it is my turn.'

'Oh, how nice. Isn't that something! I heard my mother speak of that Irish custom. Then that is why you are removing all your beautiful delph from the cabinet in preparation for house cleaning and your celebration of Mass. Have you no one to help you? You have not told me your name.'

'No, I never married. Father Brown is the only one who says I should not live alone. My name is Paddy.'

'And my name is Brigid Sullivan, the same as my mother's name. She told me that my father walked out on her and that all I have belonging to him are his beautiful dark eyes.'

Paddy found himself a chair near the kitchen table and slumped into it, sitting there dumbfounded, staring into space. Brigid looked at him in astonishment and said: 'Is there something the matter? Have I said something wrong? Have I offended you?'

Paddy arose and walked slowly to find the tin box where it lay among the delph on the table. Opening it once more, he took the letter and gave it to Brigid, saying: 'Will you please read this? Then you'll know the reason and understand why I never married.'

She read the letter quickly, and started to sob: 'This is my mother's handwriting and you are the father I have often dreamed about. I must talk to my mother in Cahersiveen.'

When Paddy had fully recovered from the shock of meeting his daughter, a warm feeling suffused his entire being. He was no longer bound by the shackles of scandal and codswallop. How unpredictable is the wheel of life. Who can foretell the secrets stored for us in the womb of the future?

Calling his daughter to his side and caressing her, he said: 'I must meet your mother without delay. In the meantime, I have to wash, shave, put on my best suit and harness my pony Rodger to the tub-trap and I can assure you when Rodger hears the whir of the wheels, the few miles from here to town will stream behind. When I am ready, Brigid, I want you to take this rug and wrap up well. I don't want you to get a chill. That would spoil everything.'

'Now that we are on our way, Paddy, can we stop at Father Brown's and let him know our intentions?'

'No, my daughter! Your mother will make the decisions from now forward. She will have the final say in the plans for her future happiness. I feel the guilty person whom she trusted. My only hope is that she does not hate me.'

Rodger was already pawing, snorting and uneasy to be off. When comfortably seated, Brigid said: 'Paddy, will you let me take the straps? I will guide Rodger.'

'Of course, Brigid, but be careful, as he responds to the slightest pressure from right or left strap. He was perfectly trained as a colt.'

'Don't worry, mother and I are good with horses, but that story can wait.'

The few miles to town were uneventful. Paddy could see how she handled Rodger. It all seemed so natural. Few words were exchanged during the short journey. An air of unpredictable expectancy as to the outcome of his meeting with his long-lost Brigid Sullivan loomed foremost in Paddy's mind. Even a crystal ball-gazing soothsayer couldn't work this one out.

'What about Father Brown and the Stations?'

'Ah, keep Father Brown out of it.'

Father Brown was different. He was a man who preached the love of Christ for all sinners. He did not pour fire and brimstone on children born outside of wedlock.

When Paddy had stabled Rodger and parked his tub-trap, the time of truth was nigh. Brigid had already sent a message to her mother to expect their arrival at the house she had rented. This was the moment when destiny was to be decided by fate or providence, call it what you wish.

Brigid said: 'Paddy, I will go in first and tell mother how I happened to find you. I know it sounds like a fairy tale but it's true, every word of it. You wait outside until I call you. It will be a gentle reunion. I'll be back shortly.'

Paddy could see that Brigid's face shone with excitement and love for her mother. He too felt for the first time the excitement of surprise and suspense spilling over him. He had to keep cool now that the unpredictable had taken reign in his life. Better to swim with the current than to struggle against it and drown. He had not long to wait. Brigid beckoned him to come and in a low whisper said: 'Take it easy, Paddy, my mother is a widow.'

This last statement left Paddy dumbfounded. He was ushered inside where he stood with hat in hand, feeling like the proverbial pillar of salt, with all his mistakes of the past written across his forehead. There she stood by the table, Brigid Sullivan: beautiful, elegant, demure, modest and shy, her dark hair showing little silver strands that made her more regal looking. The pallor of the city suited her dark eyes to perfection. Paddy was looking at a beautiful American middle-aged woman. She walked towards him like a queen with arms out-stretched. It was time to forget the past. Paddy could see teardrops glisten in her dark orbs as she led him towards the table, saying: 'Please be seated. I think we both need a drink.'

Later on young Brigid entered. The three talked late into the evening and part of the night. Brigid told Paddy how she had married John Miller, a horse trainer who owned a farm. He was a good man, a man of Christian faith and very compassionate, although not a great churchgoer. She had told him all about her daughter, and he had welcomed her into his family. It was his ambition to visit Ireland because of its famous horses. Alas, that was not to be! Tragedy struck just a year and a half into their marriage when they were seriously thinking of starting a family. He was killed instantly in a farm accident. The two Brigids had run the business until two years earlier, when it became too much for them. They decided to sell, but kept the house; both were American citizens. Eventually the mother became lonely and a yearning to visit her native country once more became an obsession; naturally young Brigid wished to see her real father.

'Now, Pat Buckley,' said the elder Brigid, 'Brigid has a bachelor father and a widowed mother. Who could ask for more?'

Paddy laughed heartily for the first time that evening.

'One more thing.' said young Brigid. 'Mother and I are inviting you to come with us to America on a prolonged holiday. She feels we need each other's company now. The outcome is still in the hands of the gods.'

'Hurray!' shouted Paddy. 'I'll pack my case in the morning.'

Then he seemed to ponder and a slight frown puckered his forehead.

'Tell us, what is the matter, Paddy?'

'The Stations,' said Paddy. 'They are announced for Saturday at eight in the morning. I have only four days to prepare. I must meet Father Brown. All the neighbours will be present, young and old.'

'Don't worry, Paddy. We will help to get the kitchen and parlour shining and also your mother's beautiful delph. We mean to have a party, a sing-song, and you will play the accordion.'

Saturday morning dawned fine and fair. Now approaching eight o'clock, the neighbours were already making sure they attended their Station Mass and paid the good pastor his yearly dues according to their means. During the celebration of Mass Father Brown delivered a little homily imploring God's blessing on his flock. He praised Paddy Buckley as the first man to help a neighbour in distress. He then welcomed Paddy's American friends who were present and hinted that Paddy deserved a long holiday from his daily work.

Brigid Sullivan, the American widow, was asked to sing a song. Approaching Paddy, who sat by the side of his daughter, Brigid laid a hand on his shoulder and sang a verse from an old ballad, 'The Bonny Irish Boy'. Everybody clapped.

What happened after that we do not know.

Ships that Pass

A sickle moon wanes
Beneath the stars
Into a sad sea
Of drowned dreams
Where tall ships slumber
In a sediment of eternity
And little waves dance
To the music of gentle zephyrs
Plucked from a harp of sea strings
To mourn their passing.

GAMES AND PASTIMES OF MY BOYHOOD

Many and varied were the games played in ancient Ireland. Hurling now takes pride of place and has reached its prime position as our national pastime. It is a game of great skill and endurance, played in almost every county in Ireland, culminating in an All-Ireland final between the best two unbeaten teams, who do battle for the McCarthy Cup before a crowd of eighty thousand people in our national stadium, Croke Park.

The crooked stick of seasoned ash is fashioned with oval or rounded handgrip; the heel, or striking part, is crooked and flat. The stick derives its name from the Gaelic word *cam-ann, camán*, meaning having a crook or twist. The best hurleys are the sticks taken from branches that have a natural twisted growth.

Many games were played with stone, such as casting a stone from the shoulder. The cast was made from a special mark. The weight of the stone varied from light to medium to heavy; three pounds, six pounds or eight pounds. The stone was usually round, clumsy and smooth, making it difficult for any one contestant to grasp. The throw or cast had to come straight from the shoulder. Any step over the line meant disqualification. It is said that activity beats strength; the muscular, brawny contestant was sometimes defeated by a lean, scrawny participant, much to the delight of the onlookers.

I remember a game called rounders being played by

the school children. I do not recall the rules of the game, but it was not unlike cricket, the English game. I heard people say that the early Irish emigrants took the game to the USA: hence the game called American baseball. I can say that the several players stood in the formation of a wide ring using a round bat or stick and, after a strike, a series of runs took place before the ball of crude, sewn leather, filled with sand or clay, was retrieved.

We played a game called 'Ducks Off', which was extremely dangerous for both spectators and participants. The ducks were pieces of round, hard stone about three or four pounds in weight. A flat table of rough stone called the granny was placed about fifty feet from the line where each throw was made. The ducks were rolled towards the flat table by a team of six boys. The boy whose stone was found to be the farthest away from the granny was obliged to place his duck on the granny, to be shot at by the other boys. A scramble would ensue for the boys to get back to the line if the stone remained stationary on the table and was not knocked off. The game had many rules and was both intricate and dangerous. The teacher frowned on it being played and punished us accordingly for taking part.

The game of 'Gobs' was played by girls with five rounded pebbles carefully selected from the bed of a stream, or gravel rounded by the action of the waves on the beach. The pebble game had many stages of skill, namely scatters, knobs, strillions and cruvs.

The leather inflated ball introduced a radical change, making football much more exciting and attractive to both players and the general public. Hurling and Gaelic football are now played at national level. Great sums of money are paid to watch the games.

Other pastimes were the hunt or the chase. The hunt for the wild boar is mentioned in sagas about the Fianna, the mythical warriors of destiny. Wild boars were found in the Glen of Prior, looking westwards on the Great Skellig. The Glen is called Gleann Orcán, *orc* being the Gaelic for boar. The stag was also hunted and became the subject of a great epic poem immortalized by Walter Scott:

> The antlered monarch of the waste
> Sprung from his heathery couch in haste.
> But ere his fleet career he took,
> The dewdrops from his flanks he shook.

The stag referred to by Scott was hunted in the Highlands of Scotland but it is interesting to note that the last retreat of the great red deer was the mountains of Kerry.

Beagle hunting has been a favourite sport in Ballinskelligs for as long as I can remember. Only the rich landlords kept kennels and packs of beagles. The local gentry kept horses at Portmagee, at Fermoyle Castle in Prior parish and at Derrynane. The terrain was not suitable for horse-riding in pursuit of the fox. Still, it was indulged in by those country squires.

The Ballinskelligs beagle clubs existed back in the 1700s. My grandfather was known as 'Tim of the dogs'. For some short time he was the kennel keeper to a certain knight squireen of the clanging hoof and horn, whose hundred dogs bayed deep and strong. My grandfather loved dogs and had a way with them. When the kennels of the Big House were opened in Portmagee, the dogs would come all the way across the mountains in the early morning to wait outside the door of his little thatched cottage in Ballinskelligs.

Gone are the halcyon days of the Big House, gone too are the masters of the hunt in creaking calfskin saddles, who plied the scourge and steel. In their stead the local peasantry still keep beagles for hare hunting. The hare-hunting beagle is a much larger breed of dog than that of the fox chase. Hare hunting is not a blood sport. The club members will not allow a hare to be killed. Rather it is an endurance test to find the best dog. When the hare is seen to falter and is showing signs of exhaustion the dogs are called off by a blast of the huntsman's horn. A closed season is declared to allow the hares to breed and bring forth their young, called leverets. It is during this period that the hunters organize a series of beagle races called drag hunts. A scent is laid down by a special set of runners over a fifteen-mile course, over moorland, mountain streams and rough obstacles. Each runner will pull a scented piece of meat or sack tied on the end of a length of rope from a starting point to a finishing gateway, where the judges await the winning beagles. The winning owners are rewarded with substantial trophies and money prizes. Some beagles are black with tan ears, said to be of the Hubert breed. Others vary in colour from speckled to blue-grey, chocolate and white. South Kerry beagles are much sought after and fetch good prices.

The following is an old poem, composed by Philip O'Sullivan, who was born in Coom, Ballinskelligs, County Kerry in 1872 and died in Saint Louis, Missouri, USA in 1959. The poem was presented to me by his son, Vincent, also from Saint Louis. It can be sung to the old Irish air of 'John and his Leather Britches'. It is named 'The Charming Beagle Hunting'.

The Charming Beagle Hunting

Come all you lads and lassies
With smiling, sporting faces,
If you but live till next year
You won't forget the races.
For races we will have,
But not for whips and saddles,
And if you're thinking that,
It's only fiddle faddle!
For Ballinskelligs is the place
Of merry sport and dancing
And chief among them all
Is the charming beagle hunting.

Trueman Lynch, ole boy,
You'd love to hear him rattle,
When Molly took the lead,
From Bolus to Duhallow.
Finder you will hear,
And with him little Towler,
He has music in his tongue,
And every cry is louder.
Fairmaid, she's the flower.
Without her they are nothing,
She keeps up the tally-ho
When all the rest are lagging.
And when the hunt is over
And you hear the bugle ringing
Ballinskelligs is the place
For the charming beagle hunting.

We took a course around
To see what dog would echo
Through Carhan's woods so fair
To the mountains of Kimego.
Valentia would resound
And Foilmore would be shaking,
Maulin yet asleep,
Kilmackerin only waking.
Johnny Lyne from Coom
With his Dido, rough and hairy,
He'd keep running with the pack,
And never yet grow weary.
So when the day is done
We'll take to sport and singing
And drink a flowing toast
To the charming beagle hunting.

SILENCE! SILENCE IN THE COURT!

Minor law cases before and after the famine were held in the magistrate's court or the court of petty sessions, usually in the local courthouse. In my locality the sessions were held in a building in Portmagee. Petty crime consisted mostly of unlighted vehicles – vehicles were classified as farm carts of all descriptions – including side carriages and tub-traps. Bicycles and motor cars had not yet arrived. Other offences brought before the courts included inebriation and disorderly conduct; wandering animals; arrears of rent; non-payment of money due; theft; trespassing; claims of malicious damage; failure to obtain dog licences; breaches of the School Attendance Act; parental neglect of children; unshod animals and poaching. It was compulsory for the owner of a farm cart to display his name and that of the townland wherein he resided on the right-hand shaft of the vehicle, in clear English lettering. Defying the edict of the Crown, my brothers printed my father's name in bold Gaelic lettering, Seán Ua Ciarmhaic, Baile 'n Sceilg. For this my father was fined ten shillings, and ten shillings was not easily come by in those days. Henceforth the name was displayed in both languages. Perhaps our ass-cart could be recorded in some book as being the first to acquire bilingual status.

Many funny tales were told of how the court and its officers operated. Country folk would attend in force to hear the pleadings presented by the plaintiff and defendant in lawsuits between neighbours. The clerk of the court was usually a minor civil servant with some scant knowledge of law. An old man from Ballinskelligs, whom people said was not the full shilling, held the conviction that he was a reincarnated lawman of some kind. He would never miss being present when the court was in session. The old man, always dressed in his Sunday best, would call for order in the court and bow to the judge. The magistrate accepted him as part of the judicial system and, to boost the old man's ego, he was provided with a special chair in the courtroom. On a day when the clerk of the court was absent, the magistrate had occasion to go to the men's room. The policeman in charge failed to quell the pandemonium that arose out of the general hubbub of loud conversation among the local neighbours, until the old man lost his patience. Rushing over to the judge's bench, taking the gavel and striking the bell, he declared in a loud voice: 'Silence! Silence in court while the barrister is pissing!' This tale I heard from old Gaelic speakers while I was yet a very young boy, from folk who could only manage the *cúpla focal* of English.

Another hilarious tale I heard from the lips of a farm-hand who was called to give evidence in a case between two neighbouring farmers. Mickey was getting on in years when I heard him relate the story, now more than seventy years ago. The aggrieved party employed him as a servant boy and farm-hand. He was called to give evidence supporting a charge of trespass, claimed to have been committed by his neighbour within the yard of the hay-barn. Mickey was called to the witness stand and cross-examined by the solicitor for the defence.

'Now, my good man, do you remember the morning

of the seventh of January?'

'I do, sir!'

'Did you notice the nuisance at the foot of the ladder?'

Mickey made no reply. The magistrate then intervened, reminding him that a witness was obliged by law to answer the question, to which Mickey replied: 'What is a nuisance, your honour?'

The magistrate said: 'Turn around and ask somebody at the back of you.'

Mickey turned and looked into the eyes of a colleague named Dan.

'What is a nuisance, Dan?'

Dan whispered behind a slanted palm: 'Something that has a bad smell, Mickey!'

One could hear a pin drop in the court. The magistrate asked: 'Do you now understand the meaning of the question?'

'No, your honour!'

'Why, Michael?'

'Because there was no bad smell, your honour!'

The magistrate spluttered and coughed and, owing to a very boisterous outburst of laughter among the peasantry, ordered the court to be cleared.

Another old story that goes back to the start of the 1800s went the rounds and was always told in Gaelic. It concerned a young man from Valentia who was purported to have raped a neighbouring farmer's daughter before joining a French fishing schooner that was shorthanded and bound for Labrador to fish for halibut and cod. It was not unusual for French fishing vessels to stop at Valentia on their way to Newfoundland. Their method of fishing was to attach baited lines to long hickory fishing rods. Dozens of rods would be arrayed in holders along the ship's side. In those days the coast of Labrador teemed with fish. It was only a matter of hauling the fish on board. Part of the crew was given to attending to the fishing rods and part of the crew to curing the fish and storing it in sealed wooden casks. When the last cask was filled it was time to return.

It seems our Sean was a long-rod fisherman, attending to several lines when required. The time to return depended very much on the Atlantic weather. The coast of Nova Scotia can be very treacherous sometimes, with thick dense fog or perhaps a freezing gale blowing from the direction of Iceland. Therefore leaving France in springtime and returning by early or late autumn was always a hazardous undertaking, fraught with danger. The trip could take ten to eleven months.

It was late autumn when Sean's ship returned to Valentia harbour. He found to his consternation that a warrant had been issued for his immediate arrest, supported by the sworn evidence of a woman who claimed he was the father of her child because of an assault on her by him at a given date. Sean was incarcerated in the local gaol pending the hearing of his case. Penalties were severe in those days. Transportation to Van Diemen's Land for stealing a sheep was a normal penalty. Who has not heard sung that beautiful Gaelic ballad of transportation, 'The Connerys'.

On the day, the trial was presided over by the magistrate at the local courthouse. As usual, the courtroom was filled to capacity. Sean's relatives and friends sat silently listening to a damning sequence of lies piling up against him, while Sean stood pale and unshaven. His fate seemed sealed until his councillor stood up in court. Asking for silence, he approached the judge, giving him a piece of paper that was an extract copied from the schooner's logbook and signed by the French captain. The document showed the date of the ship's arrival in Labrador to be one month earlier than the date the girl testified the offence had taken place. There was great jubilation in Sean's household when he was set free. It is said that his old grandmother, on hearing of his release, exclaimed in Gaelic: 'I never doubted you my grandson, you were the greatest fisherman of all, who was able to stretch his fishing rod from Labrador to Valentia!'

When I Am Free

For Mike Hammons

When I am free
I'll seek
The wonderways
Of my childhood
Far from the rapid highways
Of my manhood;

Some country lane
Where I might see
The ripening springburst
Of another summer
Glisten in the hedgerows,
And listen to twittering linnets
Within secluded bowers
Feed love
To little pulsing hearts
And open mouths;

Where I can breathe
Sweet fragrance
From the primrose,
And watch the honeybee
Take time
To kiss each lip
And sip
From yellow cups
That mingle
With wild bluebell
In the dell.

Where I can pause
A while
In peace
Until my eventide,
And watch perchance
Sweet mistress of the night
Prepare my bed,
Where I can rest
Until another dawn.

THE TALE OF THE HAUNTED PIPER

Stimulating memories fill my mind, bringing a yearning for customs of the past. Winds of change, together with the vehicle called 'mass media', provide push-button entertainment for almost every household and family circle. More than four score years and seventeen have flown since I was born. As a boy of yet tender years, I can remember sitting happily near the cosy glow of a stacked peat fire, full of tremulous, dancing flames, within the wide chimney breast of my parents' kitchen. Each night our neighbours came in their own good time and would sit in their usual places. The long winter seemed all too short. Time flew under the spell of the *seanchaí* and the saga. A discussion would usually start on topics such as farming, turf cutting, fairs, match-making, etc., often laced with humorous allusions to the sexual suitability of the couples mentioned. The womenfolk also took part in such discussions and merry banter. Weather formed an important part of the conversation.

My father, John Kirby, whose main occupation was fishing, always came under fire from a barrage of questions from small farmers interested in seasonal crop-raising: 'What do you think of the weather, John?', 'Are we in for a dry spell?' and 'Will tomorrow be fine?' Sleeping or waking, a fisherman was supposed to keep his weather eye open, reading the clouds and the telltale signs of approaching depressions. My father was a tall, well-built man, spare but muscular. His face had distinct Hellenistic features, and he wore a Moses-like auburn beard with natural whorls. In a film he would be a ready-made stand-in portraying some biblical figure. I think that because he was a fisherman he was regarded by some as the village barometer.

The neighbours were no different from any others who lived in the surrounding area, each person possessing individuality in his or her make-up. All were good-natured characters with traits of attractiveness and charm; each would show a different ability when telling a story. Some were gifted narrators, well able to catch the imagination of the listener through the captivating, beguiling power of the telling. Tomáisín Sugrue told tales of great storms, of ships in distress and roof-trees stripped in the violence of a great wind. He seemed very much at ease when relating a story, speaking in a slow, confident manner; a past master knitting detail into the fabric of his weaving. Tales of haunted houses and premonitions of tragic events foretelling disaster were all part of his repertoire. He had a wealth of information regarding the local landlords and the established order of the day. He liked to give a correct and factual account of all historical events of the past, always speaking in a beautiful, easily understood Gaelic. One neighbour in particular told the most fantastic cock and bull stories, swearing by all the blessed powers as to the veracity of each word. Tomáisín could not contain himself when listening to such rigmarole, and would object by saying in Gaelic: '*Bail ó Dhia ar an scéal gan dath!*', 'God bless the tale without colour!' or 'I would rather listen to the braying of an ass!'

My mother was the only person who had freedom of

movement during the storytelling session. She could put more peat on the fire and provide a drink of water if the need arose, or maybe a firebrand to light someone's pipe. I sometimes heard her give advice in whispering, cautionary terms to younger unmarried women who sat by the fireside, to cover their knees and stop giggling.

Storytelling was a serious business and we did not approve of any emotional distraction that might cause the *seanchaí* to lose his concentration. I listened to my father tell a strange story about a happening that took place in his grandfather's time. It was the 'Tale of the Haunted Piper'. As far as I can recollect, this was how he recounted the story handed down to him by his own father, Timothy Kirby.

'When my father Jerry arrived home from net-fishing accompanied by two other sons one late autumn night, he found not unusually that his wife Eileen O'Rahilly-Kirby had given shelter to a poor displaced person, one of many who were destitute mendicants wandering aimlessly as a result of the Great Hunger. This time it happened to be the figure of a tall, gaunt, middle-aged man, who sat in a hunched position by the dying embers of the kitchen fire. A tattered greatcoat hung loosely across his shoulders, while a set of pipes lay beside him on the long kitchen settle commonly named the rack, *an raca* in Gaelic. As Jerry Kirby was about to make conversation with the stranger, Eileen Kirby burst into the room with two younger children clinging to her side. All seemed in a very distraught state of mind. "Oh, Jerry! Oh, Jerry! We are so glad you are here," she exclaimed. "We were so frightened. Thank God you have come back."

'Trembling and shaking like a leaf, Eileen clung to her husband. Jerry Kirby stood for a moment in shock and bewilderment before turning towards the huddled figure by the fireplace and declaring in an angry voice: "Tell me, Eileen, tell me quickly, is it this rootless old vagabond who has interfered with you? If he has dared upset you I'll tear him apart!"

' "Oh, no! Jerry, no! It is the fairies or bad spirits! The house is full of them, the *púcaí* [fairy host]."

'A vacuous look of disbelief spread over Jerry's countenance. Putting his arms around Eileen he said soothingly: "Come dear, you are very confused. You must go back to bed. I fear you are developing a fever."

' "I am not sick, Jerry! You must be blind! Can you not see all our seed potatoes for next spring scattered beneath your feet?"

' "But Eileen, the seed potatoes are stored in the loft over the back kitchen."

'No sooner had Jerry uttered those words than the commotion started again. Chairs moved, delph on the dresser danced and the crouched figure by the fireside was being pelted incessantly with what was left of the precious seed potatoes. Two large balls of homemade twisted grass rope, called *súgáns,* which were in hand for securing the thatched roof next autumn, came tumbling down the ladder from the loft above, dancing and bounding precariously close to Jerry and his wife, as if thrown by a team of professional basketball players. Jerry grabbed one of the bouncing balls only, to his amazement, it was swiftly snatched from his grasp by some unseen force, and thrown violently towards the visitor sitting at the fireside. It was at this juncture that Jerry concluded that the figure by the fireside must be jinxed or harassed by some nasty poltergeist. Throwing wide the kitchen door, he decided to take action by ordering the piper to leave at once. "Please! Please! Let me stay until the dawn," said the piper, "All will be quiet then!" Jerry Kirby, being a kind and charitable man, together with his wife Eileen, kept vigil with the tormented wayfarer until morning, when all was peaceful again. They allowed him rest for some time and gave him food and alms before he travelled on. He never divulged his identity or mentioned why he was haunted by the unseen throwing spirits.'

My father also mentioned how the piper stayed the next night in a house at Ballinskelligs West, where the macabre, mysterious manifestations were experienced again. My father was a serious person who would not bother trying to unravel the esoteric. He accepted the evidence that such happenings existed and are still part of human observation.

Wild Things

I see a tender reed
Emerging from the ooze
Of cosmic sludge,
Swaying gently
In a zephyr of timelessness.
Then, behold!
A blinding, glowing orb
Surveys the scene.
The first eternal spring
Is born.
I am the nursery of life,
Warmth of my breath
Shall bid you thrive,
Bear seed
And cast again,
When autumn
Sheds the grain.
Grow sweet rush
And all wild things
Sustain.

I see a twig
Become a tree,
A bud
Become a flower,
A bird on a branch
Full of song.
Why are my ears
Deaf to music?

And my eyes
Blind to beauty
Of wild things?
Is this my Father's voice
I hear
Crash and rumble
Among darkening hills
That frown?
Is it the lightening flash
Of his loving smile
That strikes fear
Unto his children?
Who is my Father?
Am I his child,
Cast adrift
In a basket woven of reed,
Hidden among bulrushes,
Afloat
In a torrent of mystery?
Was it you,
My father's Father,
Made wild things
Happen?
An animated blob of clay!

I'll seek my place,
Within the reed-bed
Of your creation,
Where the grey heron
Stands in still waters
Of the mere,
Where silver elvers wriggle
And tall pines
Stumble and fall across

Slippery moss-clad stones,
Where sly, elusive
Water hens
Avoid intruding man.
When I sleep,
Let it be in peace,
Where blind stars of day
Become
The jewelled arch
Of my night pillow.

Lastly, I whisper a prayer.
Shepherd of my creation,
Keep my wild spirit
Within the fertile pastures
Of your fold.

MOUNTAINS: FROM CANUIG TO THE APPALACHIANS

I looked up the word 'mountain' in a dictionary: 'An elevation of the earth's surface rising abruptly, sometimes to great heights above the surrounding terrain.' The terse, sparse, economical information my investigation brought to light left me rather nonplussed. But, after all, what did I expect, having been brought up among the Kerry mountains? Did I expect some leprechaun to break into song at my elbow, singing 'The Moon behind the Hill', or perhaps 'Come Down from the Mountain, Katy Daly'? I would certainly enjoy a drop of the real old mountain dew. No, I do not relish getting bogged down with geographics or cartographics. I would much rather sing 'The Mountains of Mourne' after a few jars.

What a dull, monotonous place our world would be were it not for mountains! Who would play cowboys and Indians? There is always a thrill in expectancy, in not knowing what surprise awaits the eye behind the next mountain. It may be a beautiful gorge or ravine like Moll's Gap, leading to the breathtaking beauty of the semi-secluded, sheltered Black Valley. I hardly dare give vent to my intense enjoyment at the mountain dawn in the throes of giving birth to another sunrise. Little lakes fill with a subtle light and shadow, cast by the first rays of sunlight flooding the valley from peaks above. Waterfalls and rivulets cascade downward, taking on a silver sparkle. Near a grey boulder, mirrored in a pool, a silver trout explodes from the depths, leaving ever-widening rings on the glass-calm water, reminding me that I am not the only living organism in the so-called solitude. I sense I am being watched from a thicket, but to my great relief I am not being ambushed. As I approach the trees, a stag breaks cover and makes for the heights. Looking upwards I see the contours of the mountains. Tall peaks stand majestically in the background like humans posing for a photograph; first, second and third row.

Brian Merriman certainly knew his environment and nature in general. In his epic poem *Cúirt an Mheán Oíche* (translated into *The Midnight Court* in English by other poets, who could never do justice to the descriptive flow of the original Gaelic), the hills are described as nodding their heads as they stand overlooking one another. The colours of the countryside, the horizon, sky and woodland are all brought into play, and finally, in the introduction of that first part of his poem, Merriman says: 'If an old, emaciated person without health, home or riches could get one glimpse of the scene, it would gladden and illuminate his mind forever.'

In addition to the Black Valley, many other coombs and valleys are found within the Kerry chain of hills, none darker than the other. Sunshine does not discriminate on the grounds of language, beauty or colour. I would not expect every tourist to know the name Coom Dubh, otherwise known at the Black Valley. Fortunately I was born between the mountains and the sea. Kinnard and Canuig are only little pips at my back door, standing 1260 feet above sea level. Nevertheless, they are part of the unbroken chain encircling Ballinskelligs Bay.

Reaching southwards, these hills are crowned by Carrantuohill of the Reeks of Kerry, in a tourist route of unsurpassed beauty; a veritable altar to nature's divine artistry, called the Ring of Kerry.

Across the bay I can see the mountains of Beara, stronghold of the O'Sullivan chieftains. The great scholar An tAthair Pádraig Ó Duinín composed a poem in Gaelic in which he depicts O'Sullivan, so brokenhearted, being forced to leave his beloved mountains, beseeching the setting sun to stay a little longer:

Fóill, fóill, ariú a ghréin ghil, go leathfad mo shúil
Ar na sléibhte seo áille, mar is mór é mo dhúil
Iad d'fheiscint uair eile, fá do sholas gan cháim;
Mar, mo chruatan naoi n'uaire! Chun a bhfágtha atáim.

Stay! Stay a while, O bright sun. Cast your light
    one more time
On my beautiful hills. Great my desire
To see them once more 'neath your light without
    blemish
Ere we sever forever. Nine times more sorrow that I
    must depart.

Poets have been inspired and enthralled by mountains, and have expressed admiration for the everlasting hills. I have read about mountain climbing and loss of life on the slopes of great mountain ranges. The abominable snowman, called the Yeti, is supposed to be a man-like creature whose footprints were found somewhere high in the Himalayas. Over the years nobody seems to have seen any trace of this animal except for flat footprints with a prominent big toe. Miles up there, with nothing except deep snow, perpetually munching ice-cream cones. Poor old Yeti! It must be freezing up there! Yes, I heard that one, the story about the brass monkey.

Poets, hermits, mystics, holy men, greedy prospectors, outlaws, hunters and refugees have all been lured by mountains. On them, battles have been fought to conquer the invader or quell the madness of civil strife. The mountain has also been an ideal location for the manufacture of illicit whiskey, away from the prying eyes of the revenue man. Most travel writers weave wondrous tales of mountains and feats of intrepid, heroic, fearless adventure. Who would not be in spiritual company with a woman like Dervla Murphy in her many episodes of physical endurance, not alone along the backbone of the Andes but in other lands as well.

> Fain would I climb
> But that I fear to fall.
> If thy heart fails thee
> Do not climb at all.

Some suffer from a fear of heights, called acrophobia. The only time I got a thrill from looking down on a vast mountain range was while flying through a snowstorm from Chicago to New York in 1982, accompanied by my wife Peggy, having visited her sister in the Windy City. For a fleeting moment the sky opened. We were flying over a mountain peak of the Appalachian chain. I could see the Ohio river curling its way like a great silver serpent miles below. The snow took over again and next time we saw blue sky was on our descent to LaGuardia Airport, New York.

It was not my intention to write about saints in the first place, but I find it difficult to separate mountains from saints, especially in Kerry and other parts of Ireland as well. Slemish Mountain in Antrim is known as the mountain where Saint Patrick passed his youthful days as a slave, herding swine. Its Irish name is Sliabh Mis – the Mountain of Mis, a woman. There is another beautiful mountain in Kerry, also called Sliabh Mis. Croagh Patrick in Mayo is a place of pilgrimage, where the saint went into seclusion, spending some time in prayer and fasting away from the hurly-burly, arduous task of trying to evangelize an ancient Celtic people called Druids, who were not considered to belong to the more enlightened civilizations such as the Greek or Roman.

According to the genealogical tree taken from the Book of Leinster of the Kirbys of Munster, muintir Ciarmhaic na Mumhan, my ancestors were good practising Druids or barbarians who did not take too kindly to Christianity for some time – but that's another story. I find in the document in my possession that the Ciarmhaics had some fine Celtic names, but none from the Bible until Saint Patrick spilled water on our barbaric foreheads.

Mount Brandon, west of Tralee in County Kerry, is called after the navigator known as Saint Brendan of Clonfert. It is written that he was the son of Findlugh of the race of Ciar and was born near Tralee in the year 484 AD. It is said that he spent seven years sailing on the western seas and that he landed in various strange places. Brittany was one of the places he visited where it is said he founded a monastery.

Another beautiful mountain comes to mind, Sliabh na mBan in County Tipperary. According to folklore, on its eastern shoulder was the famous fairy palace where the Tuatha de Danann women cast a spell on Fionn MacCumhaill and his warriors. Those Tuatha de Danann women must have been up to some uncanny capers.

Who has not heard the haunting air of the ballad of 'Slievenamon' composed by Charles J. Kickham.

In dealing with saints and mountains I admit that I am not spiritual enough to attempt to unravel the secret of being a saint. Sometimes I seem to have lost sight of God on level ground. Now I am too old and feeble to climb a mountain again, I will conclude by composing a poem to show the reader I would wish to climb the mountain again. I call this poem 'Yearning'.

Yearning

I was restless.
A yearning had come
To climb the hillside
Of Canuig,
Up where silver mist
Hung curtained
On the crag,
Laced with golden arrows
From a slanting sun.

There I will listen
To red bees,
Murmuring delight,
Sipping sweet nectar
From purple heather pap.
And watch the lowing kine
Wend homeward
Across
The valley's lap.

There I will see
The hermit's rock again,
Skellig Michael
And the blue cave
Where kittiwakes complain,
Scarrif Island
And its martyr,
His gushing blood
Not in vain.

Friar Francis,
Stand and shield us
From Hades' lasting pain.

There I will rest
In the crook of the crag,
Where peace of eve
Droops dew
From heaven.
All I ask,
That time be measured
By the looping wing
Of that homeward heron.

Miangas

The previous poem, 'Yearning', is a free translation of this poem, 'Miangas', published in the collection Íochtar Trá *in 1985.*

Do bhagair sleasa na mbeanna
Ag cur glaoch orm ón ngleann,
Do chorraigh mo mhoilleacht
Is d'fhág mé faoi mhiangas trom –
Mé a bheith thuas i measc na gcarraig
Ag dreapadh na maolchlochán,
Gan eagla orm go dtitfinn
Ach spleodar im chroí agus gáir.

Ansiúd is ea a bheinn ag éisteacht
Le crónán na mbeacha rua
Ag siolpadh drúcht na meala
As cupáin fhraoigh gan stua,
Agus géimneach tréada im chluasa
Thar leabaidh an ghleanna anall
Nuais a chasfaid abhaile chun eadra
Le maolú na gréíne ag dul uainn.

Do chífinn arís Dubh-Inis
An t-oileán úd amuigh faoin spéir;
Na cuasa faoi sciatháin ghléigeal,
'Gus grágarlach na n-éan;
An foirichín go huaigneach
Ag glaoch go hard sa cheo,
Na sulairí á dtumadh féin
Is ag tabhairt a mbeatha leo.

Tógfad scíth ar an gcarraig
Go hard ar spíc an tsléíbhe,
Áit go dtiteann drúcht an tsonais
Ó ríocht gheal Flaithis Dé;
Ní bheidh suim agam in ama
I lúib na creige im shuí,
Ní bheidh miangas ar m'intinn
Ná mairg ar mo chroí.

JERRY NO NAME

Jerry was a wayward son, always in his mother's prayers. His guiding maxim was that life must be full, adventurous and merry. He was forever getting into scrapes. There was the time that a British soldier objected to his singing 'The Croppy Boy': he got his clock patched by Jerry in a fair do of fisticuffs! And, since the strong arm of authority decreed that 'thou shalt not molest, do battle with or obstruct a servant of the realm', Jerry was taken before the bewigged, bepowdered and bespectacled magistrate, his wrists clad in steel bracelets. He was handed down one month in Cork City Prison on penal labour and rations at the Queen's pleasure.

As Jerry's mother prayed fervently, a salt tear might often be seen to mingle with the prayer beads. The day of the prodigal's return she was standing by the kitchen table preparing dough for the daily bake of oven bread. As he went by the window and she spied his dark head of curls, she gave vent to a joyful mother's welcome. She threw her arms around his neck, nearly smothering him in National Pride flour.

Jerry assured his sobbing mother that he had not disgraced his parents, his family or his American relatives, and swore by all the popes in hell and friars in purgatory he would gladly do the same again to any son of a pied piper who objected to his rendering of 'The Croppy

Boy', be he bishop, knight or rook. Strong words from her little songbird whose once rosy countenance had assumed a pallor from a month on penal rations of black bread and water. After all his braggadocio he was glad to be home. He had his tender moments despite the wild streak that nature included in the mortar of his fashioning. His mother listened with warm sympathy to the tale of his sojourn in prison. He told of the day he was alone in his cell looking at the storm clouds through the bars of the prison window. Suddenly a lightening bolt hit the cubicle, leaving a suffocating smell of sulphur and a dead horse on the street outside.

'Were you afraid, son?' said his mother.

'Yes, and I was lonely. There was nowhere to go. I had lost my freedom. That was the day I wanted to come home to my parents' house again.'

'Now that you are here, we are all happy. Perhaps you will go lobster fishing with Dad or turf cutting when you recover from the effects of the prison bread on your bowels,' his relieved mother replied.

A period of peace and contentment followed, until the day when Jerry made known his intention to board a sailing vessel discharging salt at Limerick docks. The day of his departure was tearful for his mother. She was parting once again from her impetuous, wild, but much-loved offspring. Dad turned his head away, saying 'I would much rather he stayed at home. He has a wild, fearless streak in his nature. But perhaps the sea is best for him.'

Off Jerry went. He took a train from the nearest rail-head, Reenard Point, and arrived in Limerick about mid-afternoon. To his dismay, he learned that the three-masted *Mary Owens* had sailed short-handed on the morning tide. He had only the sum of five shillings. To survive, he had to spend sparingly. He had taken to himself an orphan verse without name and now had to put its philosophy into practice:

Spare not, nor spend too much, be this thy care,
Spare but to spend, and only spend to spare,
He that spends too much may want and so complain.
So he spends best that spares to spend again.

He stood at a street corner, mulling over in his mind what he should do next. That was decided for him by a strange quirk of fate. A flower girl stood before him, a neat wicker basket in the crook of her arm, full of little bunches of violets. Jerry was in no mood to buy flowers, but, it being Easter time, he gave her tuppence. She insisted on threading a few violets in the buttonhole of his jacket. Their eyes met. She was a dark-eyed, beautiful gypsy with flowing tresses and large flashing eyes. Her complexion was unusually white, unlike the typically swarthy Romany.

'Are you new in town?' she questioned.

He told her he was, and introduced himself.

'My name is Marcia Trig,' the girl said, 'My mother and I sell flowers and tell fortunes on market days. Let me read your palm.'

Jerry extended his open hand. 'Will I cross your palm with silver, so that you can tell me a lot of trash and made-up lies?'

Immediately he was sorry for his hasty remark. He saw her face light up in a flash of anger. 'Don't you dare insult me, Jerry No Name. I do not have to tell lies. The truth is written across your face. In the first place you have barely enough money to buy your dinner. Your loved ones who worry about you must be daft.'

Jerry was about to give vent to a fiery reply but

thought better and restrained his tongue. This girl's dignity held him in check.

A pony-drawn tub-trap driven by a Romany lady drew up in front of them. She was bejewelled, her eyes were as deep and dark as an eclipse of the moon and her hair was the colour of dark marble streaked with silver.

'Whoa, Randy! Whoa!' Randy came to an abrupt stop, almost dislodging the driver in a sudden forward jerk.

'Marcia! It is time to leave. Who is your man? Does he want a lift out of town? Tell him come. He looks like trouble, but you never know. He is good-looking. You found him, and maybe we'll keep him. Hah, ha!'

Jerry was no longer master of his own destiny. He was bewitched by the hypnotic power of a wandering gypsy.

Marcia came closer to him, saying softly: 'Look, Jerry from Kerry, cheer up. This is my mother. Come with us. After all it's only a hundred miles or so back to Kerry again and that's nothing to travelling people.'

Next thing he found himself sitting on one side of the tub, while Randy, head down, clip-clopped at a fast, steady trot, giving an occasional nostril-clearing snort, tossing his head as he sped countrywards. Marcia and her mother conversed in a tongue Jerry had never heard, a Romany dialect called Shelta, a mixture of old Gaelic and Indo, still used by nomadic tribes who sometimes congregate for reunions at Epsom Downs in England.

On reaching the outskirts of a town the tub turned sharply into a narrow country lane that led to the dry floor of a disused quarry. The circle of high rock walls gave shelter and privacy. Randy knew every step and, shaking his lovely piebald mane, came to a full stop. Standing in the quarry was a gaily-painted wagon with a high round roof, an excellent vehicle with the wheels shod in steel and rubber. A large, speckled grey mare cropped the grass among rocks in the far corner of this seemingly no man's land. Jerry thanked his benefactors for the lift and said: 'I'll be on my way for Kerry.' However, Marcia and her mother Paula insisted he stay: 'No! Jerry No Name, you must rest. Even travelling people must sleep and eat.'

He was now introduced to Marcia's father, Heron, a tall man, tree-like, broad-shouldered, raw-boned yet muscular, well beyond the half-century and clad only in an apology for a shirt. Turning, he fixed a dreamlike gaze on Jerry with his eyes of steely blue. This man was strange to Jerry. He was nature's enigma, trained to enjoy the ebb and flow of the changing seasons, born in winter, leafing in spring, flowering in summer and sleeping in autumn. Heron was a man who had learned from the flush of eve, from the deep of night and the burst of dawn, who could stroke the silver salmon from the pool beneath the falls and tickle the belly of the brownie for breakfast or snatch a cock from its roost in the trees. Who better than he could measure the hop of a buck rabbit or peg down a snare? He was standing near a pot of savoury stew that hung from an iron tripod suspended over glowing coals.

It did not take any persuasion for Jerry to stay. The sweet aroma of the meat stew filled the calm evening air and he felt ravenously hungry. Heron addressed him: 'You are welcome to our company. Stay as long as you like, until you feel ready to go. So come, let us eat.'

The party had comfortable seats made from old packing cases. Jerry took a seat across to a large rock and sat alone. Paula filled four tin basins with stew, and he relished every spoonful. Marcia presented him with a steaming mug of tea and slices of buttered baker's loaf. He thanked his generous friends and told them he wished he could repay their kindness. They said he could stay for a while, that they liked his company, and that that was all the payment they required.

As the evening wore on a visitor arrived at the quarry, a local farmer by the name of John O'Brien, a thickset man with a pair of arms like clubs and gnarled, ham-like fists, fingers half-open, half-closed. The muscles of his neck from his jaw to his shoulders resembled an upturned bucket. He was like a circus strongman or a Samson who had extricated himself from the Old Testament. Walking up to Heron who sat near the campfire, O'Brien spoke first: 'The boys told me you were here. You went away last time without paying for the hay, Gypsy Heron.'

'Yes sir, I did! That was a wet morning. Herself was feeling sick and we had to move sudden, but I didn't forget. A gypsy will never forget. He always comes back, sir. I brought your Missus the rug from over yonder. She wanted a rug from there, sir. Have you got the grey yet?'

'I have, Heron. That is why I came to see you, not about the hay.'

'I'll pay for the hay, sir. Four bales it was.'

'Forget about the hay, Heron. The grey is off her feed and losing weight. Her foal is not thriving. Come up to the stable and have a look at her.'

'Why don't you bring a vet?'

'No, Heron. You were born with a horse in your bedroom. You know more about horses than any vet I know of. Get your jacket and come.'

Heron took his jacket and as John O'Brien was about to leave he jerked his head in Jerry's direction,

remarking: 'He's not one of your kind. Why is he here?'
Jerry stood with his back against the quarry wall, his
arms folded. O'Brien approached him, saying: 'Hello,
young man. What is your name and where do you come
from?'

'My name is Jerry and I come from Kerry.'

John O'Brien laughed lightly: 'Ah! Sure they have no
farmland in Kerry.'

'That's what you think, Mr O'Brien. We had so
much land in Kerry we had to pile it up to make room
for it.'

'Are you a tinker?'

'No. I wish I was a tinker, a tinsmith or a tradesman.'

'Why are you here then, if you are not one of the
travelling class?'

'That's my business, Mr O'Brien.'

O'Brien was already losing his cool: 'Don't get
cheeky with me, young man!'

'I am only answering your questions. I missed the
boat. I was to sail this morning and the gypsy man gave
me food. I often saw you at the yearling fair in Cahersiveen and at the horse fair at Puck. It was there you
bought the grey mare from Mike Galvin. You don't
make friends very easily, Mr O'Brien, and every cock
crows loudest on his own dunghill. Perhaps you might
travel to Kerry again and buy a few calves from me?'

John O'Brien looked long and hard at Jerry. It was
evident he was taken aback. 'Can you milk a cow, Jerry?'

'I can.'

'Where did you learn?'

'On my father's farm I milked all kinds. I cured
inflamed udders. I took warts from teats. I tamed kick-
ing cows and cows that would not yield milk. I would
milk anything with a tail and four legs on it. In fact, I'd

go as far as saying that I would milk a wild cat going through a skylight.'

John O'Brien's countenance changed. A smile flickered across his broad face. He laughed heartily. Jerry was relieved that he had touched at least some humorous chord in him. Heron stood immobile, head down, silent-tongued, unemotional, uninterested, or perhaps carefully listening to the play.

'Would you come and work for me, Jerry?' said John O'Brien.

'Thank you, sir, I'll think about it. Now I feel I must go home to Kerry.'

O'Brien stepped up to Jerry, extended his hand and shook Jerry's, saying: 'If ever you wish to work for me I'll gladly employ you. The man I hired last is with me for twenty years and that's not a bad record.' Turning to Heron he continued, 'Come gypsy, let's see the mare.'

Suddenly Jerry felt a strong urge to hit the road. He would walk by night and sleep in the hedgerows by day. But first he had to say goodbye to Marcia and her parents who had been so kind. It was not easy to head back to Kerry again. A soft whispering voice broke the silence of his reverie.

'Serious thinking, Jerry No Name?' Marcia said.

'Yes, Marcia, very serious. I feel I must go now.'

She slipped an arm through his and stood very close. He could feel the warmth of her body. My God, she smelled good! Her perfume was of wild bluebells and honeysuckle. He forgot she was the flower girl with the violets to whom he had offered tuppence.

'Yes,' she said sadly. 'I suppose you must go. I see a long, brown dusty road winding around brown and hazy blue hills. I see cliffs, seabirds and islands. I see sadness, love and loneliness, also a little trouble.'

'Stop! Stop! Do not try to read the future. You think you have power but it will only bring me bad luck.'

'You are unhappy, Jerry. Is that not so?'

'Yes, Marcia, that is so. I am not free to do as I wish. I have no money, no work, no food, no friends. Only the sky, the air and the waters are free.'

'Is not that enough freedom, Jerry? You say you have no friends. That is not true, Jerry No Name. Even dogs love their friends. Think before you hit the road south.'

He remained silent for some moments before he spoke again: 'You are my true friends and I do not wish to lean on your hospitality. That is why I must go tonight.'

'I know why you want to go. If you stayed with the travelling people it would hurt your false pride, Jerry No Name.'

'No, no, you have it all wrong!'

'What then? Did the farmer make you feel uneasy?'

'Maybe so, I didn't like him.'

'I do not like his kind either, Jerry. Maybe it's because a rich farmer tried to rape me once. He had three farms and a wife of his own. I got the better of him by threatening I'd tell my father. And also this, if I had to use it,' she said, pulling from under her dress a short, broad blade of shining steel. 'Look, Jerry, I'll show you. I can stick this deep in a tree at fifty yards. Anyway, I never told Dad about the attack. The farmers respect Heron the Gypsy. Dad would kill anyone who might hurt me. Oh yes, I told Mama. She is great. People come to her who lose things and ask for advice on buying land or getting married, and she is never wrong. We never tell fortunes locally. The priest does not believe we have gifts. Of course some fortune-tellers are only fakes. Is there a woman in your life, Jerry?'

'No, Marcia.'

'Do you like girls, Jerry?'

'I suppose I do, Marcia.'

'Had you a lover, Jerry?'

'What do you mean, Marcia?'

'Had you a girl that you kept company with?'

'Look here! Stop quizzing me like an old woman in confession. I am no more a saint than you are a reverend mother. Love, courting and kissing are all part of human emotion. Even the birds and the bees know that, Marcia. Have you ever seen guillemots make tender love on the crag of Skellig Michael?'

'What is a guillemot, Jerry?'

'A wild unbridled bird of nature like yourself, Marcia.'

'Where did you get all the fine words? Mimicking the gentry I suppose. You'd do well at a horse fair beating the dealers at their own game. I can hear remarks like "Here comes the gypsy with the golden tongue." Some day you'll build me a house with cornerstones of golden words and a rooftree of love!'

'Marcia, you are a rogue!'

'Why, Jerry No Name? Because you are using the language of poets and nearly all poets are rogues. I was sent to school in Hungary where poets were very poor like the Irish. Come, you must see our wagon. Look, Mama is waiting.'

Paula greeted Jerry at the half door. He slipped off his boots and left them on the shelf outside. The interior had plenty of headroom and was lit by a brass oil lamp with a crystal prism glass-shade, shedding a soft white light. All was spotlessly clean. The folding table was carved and had many uses, including games such as chess. It was a fixture, like the metal stove, which was only used in winter. A little rack, like one seen in churches, held a collection of books. Some titles had to do with horses, some with herbs and cures, and some with music. Several brass ornaments, pictures and carvings were attached to the side-walls. A beautiful icon of Christ suspended in a multicoloured cloud hung beside a painting of the black Madonna on the opposite wall. The floor and seats had bright oriental rugs, giving the room a welcoming cosiness. Sleeping quarters were at the rear.

'Mama, Jerry is leaving us tonight.'

'No, Marcia, Jerry is not leaving. We had a son, Ivan, like you, Jerry, with the same dark eyes and the same dark curls. I remember the day he was killed on the way home from market, when he fell from Grandpa's grain cart. You were here before, but then your name was Ivan. Let me see you smile like him. You are born again, so you won't leave yet, Jerry. A window I thought was sealed forever is opened again. So let's drink some wine and play music.'

It was at this point that Heron returned. He applauded from the steps outside, saying: 'You have a great gift, young man.'

They all sat late into the balmy summer night, until Heron decided it was time to prepare for rest. He said: 'The small tent is pitched beside the shelter of the rock and the womenfolk have prepared your bed. Before you retire, I have a few words of advice to give you. It is a free education if you care to listen. Your repartee with John O'Brien a few hours ago did not impress me, though I must say you held your own. O'Brien is a rich farmer and a very impatient person who thinks only of land, crops, work and grass, but despite that he is a fair man to deal with. You are both hot-tempered and bad listeners. The red man of the plains is a wise person. He listens to the wind, even when it sweeps in fury across the hills or whispers in gentle zephyrs through the valley. He listens to the trees, the rustle of leaves, the breaking of twigs, the movement of animals, the singing of birds, a splash in the stream, a cricket in the grass, the growl of thunder, the plop of a raindrop, a hundred and one spoken words of nature, each with a message and a meaning. Man is a product of nature and nature is a product of the mysterious miracle we call the Eternal Father or God. Other words of advice are as old as the hills. Do not spread your cloak on more ground than it will cover. Do not seek revenge. Do not cast suspicion on the innocent. Do not turn your back to good advice. Do not make enemies. Do not forsake those who have helped you. Do not burn the roof that sheltered you, in case you may want to return. Examine the ford before you attempt to wade the torrent. And most of all, look for peace first within yourself and next in your companion. The circus man must be free from the fear of falling before he can walk the tightrope. Peace of mind will relax the tensions of the body. So goodnight, Jerry, and sleep well.'

Jerry went to the tent by the rock and crept in between warm blankets laid on a pallet of straw. Drawing the flap of the tent he shut out the night. Tired and disappointed, he did not have the peace of mind that Heron spoke of. He had to try to avoid the temptation of staying here. He could never adapt to the life of the travelling people. A nomad is specially born for the road of every dawn, and he was not of their kind. Having slept for some time, he awoke feeling chilly. Hurriedly, he pulled on his clothing, and, taking his boots in hand, he tiptoed stealthily across the quarry floor.

The night had stars lit only by the dim, waning

moon-sickle on the horizon. Jerry decided he would climb across the quarry face at its lowest point into the bawn field at the back, where he could disappear without trace or fear of detection. So far, so good. He passed by the caravan and the low point of the quarry where the mare was tethered. The animal whinnied gently, then neighed loudly. Hearing Heron cough somewhere near the caravan, Jerry decided he must make a run for it. He climbed up into the jagged rocks that bit the soles of his feet. If only he had left his boots on!

When he stood on the rim of the quarry he could see the fields beneath and the forms of cattle resting in the dim moonlight. Peering downwards, he estimated the drop to be ten or twelve feet. He flung the boots down and heard them bounce on hard ground. This was his escape route. What he did not realize was that Heron was listening to his every movement and saw him silhouetted against the sky. Heron shouted: 'Hold on! Don't jump! It's twenty feet of a drop. It's too dangerous.'

When he thought about the events of that night, Jerry concluded that he must have panicked and taken the 'sheep's jump' into the abyss. Later, he would remember landing heavily among rocks before the lights went out on him – mercifully. When at last he gained consciousness he could see the shaded oil-lamp and hear a whisper in the distance. His head ached like a split pea. When he opened his eyes he was able to discern Heron's face, and realized that he was being offered spoonfuls of water. Jerry soaked in every precious drop, like some wilting plant deprived of moisture. Later, Heron fed him milk and some other potion. Jerry's whole body ached, especially his head. He felt sick and sore. Again he fell into a very deep sleep, and when he again came to, bright lights were everywhere. His first instinct was to sit upright and leave the bed, but he was restrained by a woman who told him: 'No, Jerry, not yet. You have been very sick.'

The bright light dimmed and came on again at intervals. Then all went blank again. It must have been a long time before Jerry awoke again. He heard someone whisper in a low voice that seemed to come from a very faraway place: 'Time to wake, Jerry!'

This time Jerry sat bolt upright. The summer sun was streaming shafts of warm sunlight across the fixed table where Marcia, Paula and Heron were having breakfast. He was on the pallet on the far side of the caravan. They immediately turned their attention to Jerry, telling him to lie back and take it easy. He did not argue. He was much too weak. Marcia brought a large mug of tea and a little slice of toasted bread. Placing one arm around him, she murmured. 'You fool! You nearly ruined everything and all but killed yourself into the bargain.' Jerry made an effort to undo the bandage on his head, which up until now he had been totally unaware of.

'Oh no, you don't touch the bandage, Jerry. It will have to stay in place until Doctor Daly sees you again tomorrow. He put twenty-seven stitches across your stubborn coconut. You have been in another world, Jerry. For three days the doctor was afraid you might not wake up. You bled like a stuck pig.'

'How can I thank you all?'

'You can thank us by not being so stubborn. Heron and my mother have words to say to you. They want you to stay with us for a while. I will not tell you more just yet, until you promise not to run away in the night again.'

'I promise, Marcia, but don't you understand we are

poles apart?'

'You are wrong, Jerry. We are not poles apart, we are just travellers through life, both of us in search of the same horizons. John O'Brien came to see if you wanted to milk his cows next morning. We told him you had an accident, hit by a loose stone, which fell from the quarry. He is not so bad after all. He came by again today with milk and eggs. You did not look as if you would recover at that stage. I saw only one other person as pale as you were. He was a horse dealer who lay like a snuffed-out wax candle on the altar of death for four long days, after being torpedoed by a clout from a hames-wielding Amazon maiden whom he tried to have forced love with.'

'Marcia, you speak sometimes as if butter wouldn't melt in your mouth, and yet you speak of violence as if it were something to boast about.'

'No, Jerry, the violence I speak of is the violence of survival. If the Amazonian had not wielded the hames, she would have been savagely ravished by the horse dealer. Nothing has changed, Jerry. This world is vanity and a chase after the wind. Now you must rest and recover your lost energy.'

Heron and Paula came and told Jerry how anxious they were during the time he had lain unconscious and that Doctor Daly would see him to give his final verdict. Jerry must have dozed and was awakened by the doctor. After a series of pressure tests to his head, the doctor said he was pleased with his state, but that Jerry was still suffering from a concussion, which would wear away slowly.

As the days passed he slowly felt better. He remembered his Gaelic-speaking grandmother likening health to a bird with a dozen wings, in a hurry to fly away and when returning seeming to fly slowly on only half a wing. How true, he thought! He struggled not to entertain self-pity; he realized that he was entangled in a web woven from his own stubborn impetuosity. Here lies the man who missed the boat, he thought.

By the end of the week Jerry was feeling much better and was able to sit out in the sun for a few hours. Marcia often sat near him. One day she asked: 'Do you like being here, Jerry?'

'No, Marcia. I feel I should not be causing so much hassle for you good people.'

'That shows you want to be your own man and you have concern for others. I know a little more about you each day. You are big-hearted, caring, but also proud. Do you like me, Jerry?'

'Yes, Marcia. I like you, the same as I like your father and mother. You have all been so kind to me.'

'Do you like me better than the beautiful dark-haired girl you carry around in the inside pocket of your jacket?'

'So you rifled my pockets, Marcia? Shame on you!'

'No, no, Jerry! Not so fast. It was urgent that I wash your jacket, as it was soaked in blood. Don't you think it was right for me to salvage anything that might have been destroyed in the washing? Well, here is her photo. Do you love her, Jerry?'

'I love her very much and not a day goes by but I worry about her. She is my mother, Marcia, and this is a picture of her taken before I was born. She is beautiful, and you remind me of her. She is so caring, just like you.'

'I showed the picture to Mama and Dad. They understood the reason you were running away more clearly now. But when they come to know the picture is of your mother, they will want you to stay a while longer. Did my father discuss the sea with you?'

'Yes, he asked me questions about the sea, which set me wondering, coming from a travelling gypsy man.'

'Yes, Jerry! My father sometimes will talk about strange things, more so lately. But even if his questions seem ridiculous, do not try to cross him. You see, we are gypsies, but of a different kind. We have a link with the sea. Heron's father was a sea-captain and his wife was born in Nova Scotia of Irish and Hungarian blood. Heron grew up on board his father's whaler. It was in Labrador he met Mama. She has Quaker blood in her. My mother is a good woman. Are you listening, Jerry? Lately Dad seems to talk very nonsensically about the sea. He dreams of long voyages but we know in our hearts this is not real. Dad is a sick man, but at the moment that is all I can tell you. Do you trust me, Jerry?'

'I do not know what to make of you or your parents. Perhaps you are a scheming, cunning lot! Will you walk into my parlour, said the spider to the fly? Marcia Trig, you can tell your spiders that they will not make a meal out of this little fly.'

'Oh, Jerry, you are so unpredictable. My father and mother are wise in the ways of the world. You must learn to trust us. Come, let us go to the waterfall. I'll bring the trout rod.'

On the way she talked about the wonderful art of fly-fishing, and was eager to teach Jerry all about it. She knew everything about tying flies and making them resemble the real thing in colour, shape and size. Some she made from the glossy blue-green feathers got from the starling's wing and some from its speckled breast feathers. Other lures she built from the tail feathers of the brown wren and some from the two head feathers of the crested green plover that we call *pilibín* in

Gaelic. It was delightful watching her cast on the slow-moving water at the head of the pool, making the fly fall gently on to the glossy surface, softly and light as a speck of thistle-down, allowing it to drift on the gentle flowing current, towards the widening circle caused by a feeding trout.

To please her, Jerry tried to follow her every instruction, but somehow the fly fell everywhere but on the desired spot. She praised his effort, saying playfully: 'Jerry, if you ever catch a trout it will be because he gave himself up. Another hundred lessons, one per day and you'll be an expert.' Jerry was careful to watch her every movement with admiration and some envy. It all seemed so easy. The fly was sent out over the water, stooping, circling, dipping and dancing like the seed of dandelion fluff doing a tiptoe ballet across the polished surface of the pool. The ensnaring, enchanting skill was repeated, but this time it touched the water. Then came the flash, splash and break with the quick curving of the rod and the song of the reel. To her it was only a job to be done. No excitement, no impatience, the tight sway of the line. Every time there happened a reach or rush, Marcia quickly recovered any loop of slack, stepping from one tussock to another near the brink of the pool. She deftly guided her stricken captive into the reed shallows.

The sun had now gone off the stream and fish were seen to rise in all directions, so Marcia changed flies once more, reverting to a less sporting way of fishing, the swing-and-land method. The moment a trout took, she swung the fish to the bank. It was a quick way of getting fish for supper. In all, the pair had a dozen fine trout of varying weights. Jerry felt more excited than Marcia as they walked the half-mile quarrywards. There was so much to be admired in this mysterious woman of the seasons.

On reaching the caravan they were heartily welcomed by Paula and Heron, as if they were away for a long time. Marcia was kissed by her mother and Heron shook her hand. Jerry found that he felt embarrassed with the warmth of feeling. Maybe he did not understand some aspects of their traditional culture, or maybe he was not willing to share an outward show of loving emotion. Was he too shy or perhaps too backward? Did he fear being called 'sissy', or was he just cold, unloving and ignorant? The display of affection helped him to do some plain thinking about his own temperamental behaviour.

After the meal, Heron bade him goodnight and went to his bed. Paula broke down and wept, and Marcia tried to comfort her. Jerry was astounded, and blurted out: 'What's going on?'

'Jerry,' said Marcia, 'Three years ago Dad had a brain tumour removed that was malignant. Now the roots are active again. Dad is a good man. Doctor Daly says it's only a matter of time and that we should remain here for a month or more. We feel when he dies we will be very much alone. That is why we wanted you to stay in the first place, and we should have told you of our intentions before now. Travelling people that we know well would only be too glad to stay with us, but Heron would not have them. Heron the Gypsy is proud, Jerry, but he has accepted you. We know he likes you. Do you remember when he saw you on that first night, he told you to stay as long as you liked? We were amazed. When we offered you a lift we had nothing else in mind, but in a short space of time we grew to like you. Now we have told you all and you are free to leave. There are no bonds to bind you, no manacles to burst, no locks and no iron bars. We will not beg of you to stay. Remember, we also are smeared by the sin of pride. All we ask is that you make your own decision and when you have considered you will let us know before you say goodbye. Now, let us sleep. Remember the old saying: "Do not take the leap of the sheep from the cliff top and examine the ford before you attempt to wade the torrent." Goodnight, Jerry No Name.'

Next morning broke bright and fair. Jerry was out at sunrise listening to the lark climbing its ladder from the meadow and scattering pearls from the dewy counterpane of the dawn. Each throatful of its song was an inspiration for him in making a decision. He was conscious of a hand stealing gently into the crook of his arm. Marcia's voice was a mere whisper: 'What are you thinking of?' Jerry kept looking up into the blue sky watching the bird ascending. 'I am stealing the lark's song and composing a poem for you, Marcia:

> I shall hie with the gypsy maiden,
> To the pool beside the lea,
> Where silver trout weave widening rings,
> In darkening hush of eve,
> There shall she ply her magic,
> Making the lure dance free,
> For the spell of the gypsy maiden,
> Is enslaving the soul of me.

'Last night you said I would become expert at trout fishing after having a lesson a day for one hundred days. I am taking my first lesson tomorrow. If I am not an expert maybe we will extend the time to another hundred days. And who knows what will happen then. At least we will not be apart for two hundred days!'

The Fishing Witch

The Fishing Witch,
Awaits beside the river,
Where widening circles rise,
From out a shadowed pool.
The tackle of her trade
Dark sorceress prepares,
Some ghoulish furry things,
With venom in their wings.
Raising her magic rod,
Above the water,
Abracadabra!
She makes her ploy,
How deft she drops
The mocking lure,
Light as thistledown,
To dance its deathly ballet.
Within the telltale circle.
A lightning silver flash,
And splash!
The barb strikes home.
Alas, too late.
The flurry to escape!
The foolish hour has come,
The sibyl's work is done.

Bathing Beauty

I walked the rustic shore of Boolakeel,
Rude habitat of cormorant and seal.
The everlasting hills were fair to see,
The crags, the caves, the inlets of the sea.

And as I stood on cliff-top looking down
On gentle waters where giant shadows frown,
My gaze in a sheltered cove it did intrude
To see a bathing beauty in the nude.

There she lay like Eve at dawn of time
With ne'er a fig leaf, save the salt sea brine,
Nor silken robe her nymph-like frame adorned,
As naked as a chill September morn.

Her flaming tresses did the waves unfold
And wafted to and fro like fronds of gold.
Her milk-white breasts above the wavelets show,
Pink-tipped like rose-strewn petals on a snow.

She gambolled, pirouetted and she spun.
A leaping salmon too enjoyed the fun.
An otter dived to close his watery hatch,
Perhaps he thought it was unfair to watch!

I read of holy David being a fool,
Who summoned the young maiden from the pool.
I cupped my eyes lest I should let lust in,
And be left like him, remorseful for my sin.

PISEOGA: OLD SUPERSTITIOUS BELIEFS

'Ná cum geas agus ná bris geas.'
'Do not make a spell or do not break a spell.'

Superstition is not the birthright of any one ethnic group within the human race. Irrational belief in omens, charms, talismans, etc. exists in even the most enlightened of established orders. Belief in the occult and fear of the unknown is an entrenched legacy we can be accused of having inherited from our Druidic antecedents of Gaul, Britain and Ireland.

When did superstition start? Who knows? Perhaps millions of years ago. Was it when Homo erectus first stood on his hind legs, shed his tail and gazed in wonder at the stars? If traditional customs are to be altered, suppressed or prohibited, they must be replaced by something more valuable and praiseworthy. The dawn of Christianity in Ireland set the collision course between the new and the old in their search for a supreme being. We visualize Saint Patrick coming face to face with a proud people of common ancestry who worshipped fire and water. What did it take to convince a so-called people that he, Patrick, had made contact with the source of man's imaginative yearning, a figure who had emerged from the Stygian gloom declaring He was the Son of God? The residuum of Druidic belief now became mixed in a lesser way with the early Christian Church. Hard and fast tenets of many thousand years of the old order could not be changed suddenly. Little fragments of their customary life remained with us, even into the early part of the last century.

Black magic and extraordinary, weird power can stem from direct communication with evil, and limpets of the old leaven and still cling to the armour of light. Superstition spanned all of life, from birth to burial. The time of birth related to the phases of the moon and tides, which in turn were signs of future failure or fortune. An offspring born with a caul was supposedly lucky, a caul being only a fragment of the membranous tissue from the expelled placenta, sometimes found attached to the head. This dried and preserved piece of withered tissue is still kept by many deep-water seamen as a talisman against drowning. This belief is old hat but to this day is found to exist among sailors on the seven seas.

'Happy is the corpse that the rain rains on!' Pagan ritual connected with death is still observed in many countries. Death masks and splendour were the hallmark of the Pharaonic kings of Egypt. Letting buzzards pick the bones of the dead was the pathway to heaven for certain tribes among the Tibetan mountain peaks. The natives of some Polynesian islands practised the straightening of the bones at a shrine facing from north to south. The early Irish used cremation, as in India. The funeral pyre was used in the form of burning ships in ancient Greece and in other Eastern countries. In pagan Ireland the corpse was sometimes pelted with pieces of hard peat while it lay in its death shroud. This was a show of disdain for the Grim Reaper, who was thought to be present in the dead. The custom of taking the remains to the cemetery was by the longest route possible. The shortest route was for food. The old saying in Gaelic was: '*Timpeall chun an teampall agus an cóngar chun an bia.*' People were careful not to stumble or fall to the ground in a graveyard. It was considered most unlucky.

In parts of England, the well-off country folk had very expensive and odd funeral rites. Hired mourners called mutes were dressed in black silk suits, white cravats and tall stovepipe hats, black patent leather shoes, white stockings and gloves. The faces of the mutes were done in a white cosmetic, with red lips and black eyebrows. The hearse carriage was black with ornate glass doors and sides engraved and gilded, pulled by four white or ebony-black horses complete with two drivers and two footmen who rode on the hearse, resplendent in their livery. The harness of the horses shone with gleaming brass buckles and polished creaking leather. The horses had plaited and dressed manes. The long whips were made of white woven leather. The four mourning mutes walked immediately behind the hearse, two abreast, always looking straight ahead. Tall men who were matched in stature, their hands joined in front with arms extended and fingers pointing heavenwards, as if in solemn prayer. These hired mourners were forbidden to speak or even glance to right or left. They were to act the part of living death in the solemn duty they were hired and paid for.

Some sixty years ago, a friend from Yorkshire related the following story to me. A funeral cortège with full ritual trappings wended its way to a country churchyard. The hearse arrived at an acute bend where two roads met on a country lane leading to a farm. It was at this point only a short time previously that a farm wagon carrying a load of foul animal manure had spilled some of its contents to a depth of some inches on to the roadway. As the cortège proceeded, the mutes suddenly found themselves ankle-deep in filthy animal excrement. George and Bill were the first two mutes walking solemnly beside each other. Sniffing the air upon perceiving the foul smell, George ventured to break with the observed rules of silence by giving Bill a quick elbow dig in the ribs, to which Bill responded from the side of his closed lips: 'Wot?' Whereupon George retorted in a low voice: 'Can you smell, Bill? The bugga must 'ave busted.'

Keening comes from the Gaelic word *caoineadh*, meaning lamentation, expressing sorrow for a death. The *corónach* was the dirge and also the war-music of the Gallóglaigh, the Scottish foot soldiers. The Irish *bean sí* was woman of the fairy host. Our earliest colonists introduced this belief to Ireland, which seems characteristic of the Celtic race. The wailing woman, a banshee, forewarned many Milesian families of approaching death or disaster. Cliodhna was the powerful banshee who ruled the airy spirits of south Munster. Keening the dead is no longer practised; mourning has now become a more personal matter.

Witchcraft is still practised in many countries. Covens are still in existence in many parts of Britain, as part of a religious cult. Jesus was crucified as a blasphemer and when He had risen from the dead was proclaimed a king by His tormenters, who said: 'He is indeed the Son of God.' The Maid of Orleans was burned at the stake as a witch and later was canonized a saint, thereby giving us a burned witch as a saint. Seemingly the Church itself found it difficult to determine between good and evil influence.

Superstition takes on a more sinister role when used

with evil intent to harm another person, his goods or property. Placing rotten eggs, bones of diseased animals etc. on a neighbour's property was part of the black art carried out by people caught in the web of the occult, invoking and having recourse to diabolic power. Perhaps some did not fully understand the powerful, malevolent influence they wielded against their neighbours. Therefore it is fitting to say, in the simple words of the paternoster: 'Lead us not into temptation, but deliver us from evil.'

I remember hearing about all the old little superstitions, which had mostly vanished in my time. How unlucky it was for a fisherman to be accosted by a red-haired woman on his way to the harbour! A fox, a hare or a priest was also taboo. The worst wish you could give an angler was to say to him: '*Madra rua ar do bhaoite!*' meaning, 'A fox on your bait!' A salmon was referred to as *an duine uasal* (the gentleman) when spoken of in an angling boat. Seamen were in dread of storm petrels coming aboard their ship as harbingers of foul weather and disaster; of sailing on Friday, especially the thirteenth; of omens and signs such as stars in the path of the moon – in fact there was a whole litany of dos and don'ts. Monday was not considered a fit day to start a project. Digging a grave should be avoided if possible by spading the first sod of soil on Sunday. Sheep-shearing or hair-cutting on Monday must also be avoided. '*Luan scrios ort!*' was the ugly form of a Gaelic curse, meaning that Monday's devastation might fall on you. '*Lomadh an Luan*', all cutting on Monday, was taboo.

My parents never paid any attention to the old superstitious beliefs, so I didn't have any hang-ups, although I was sorely tempted on my wedding morning. I lived alone for some time before I married, and several weeks prior to my wedding a fine dress shirt took fire as a result of a cigarette burn. My aunt Nell said it was a sure sign I would marry soon. Burnt holes in my shirt, she said, were fulfilling the words of the old *piseog*: *Comharthaí pósadh poilleanna dóite.* The last thing I did before going out to meet the car that was waiting to bring me to the bride's house was to accidentally smash a fine mirror into forty-eleven pieces. Alas! poor Yorick, seven years of bad luck! And as if some vicious imp from the netherworld decided to taunt me still further, as I stepped into the cold January dawn, there, obstructing my pathway, hopped a lone magpie. 'One for sorrow!' At that juncture I decided I must look for help, by making a fervent sign of the cross and saying: 'Deliver me from evil, dear Lord, before going forth to meet my doom.' Peggy and I had no old slippers thrown after us, no confetti, no tin cans tied to our car and no soppy speeches. We all ate and drank in plenty and naturally made merry. I can't remember having heard anybody saying to me that morning: 'Something old, something new, something borrowed, and something blue.' But despite all the broken mirrors and hopping magpies, the marriage is still sound sixty years later!

Sea Magic

O, bitter sea
Of green froth spume,
Brimming, breaking, spilling,
Swirling, foaming, roaring,
Yet in my soul
I love you!
Now, calm sea,
Kissing, waving, lapping,
Turning and washing
Blue pebbles
On the shore,
Still I love you more.

Why do my thoughts
Mingle with
The curling, waving weave
Of your magic spell
That makes me part of you?

THE NIGHT HAUL AT BOLUS

Sean and myself were busy preparing our lobster pots for the night haul, a slow business requiring time and patience. Some pots needed repair after being savaged by some huge conger eels, who, finding themselves trapped, had bulldozed their way to freedom, leaving behind torn ends and wrecked lathing. And of course it was most important that all torn and missing baits were replaced. Lobster pots fall prey to many predators on the scrounge for the bait that was only intended to attract lobster and crayfish. Yet man has failed to devise an effective plan to deal with these freeloading, uninvited guests.

When the gear was ready, we set the pots carefully in selected places, sometimes near a sunken reef or the dark, deep side of a sheltered cave. Then we cast our mooring stone in the shelter of Faill an Reithe, the Cliff of the Ram. We carried a large iron pot three-quarters filled with gravel, on which we built our fire of peat. I got ready nice cross-chunks of fat red bream, first removing the heavy silvery scale. This I cooked in a gallon can made of gleaming white tin that had formerly held boiled sweets called bullseyes. The cans were readily available when empty at any grocery store and were very good value for sixpence. We kept two tins, one for boiling fresh water and the other for cooking meat or fish. The water container was an oval oak keg, which wouldn't roll with the movement of the boat as a barrel would. Sean brewed some excellent tea, half a gallon in all. We ate several slices of buttered, homemade griddle bread. The butter was also home-churned with little droplets of fresh buttermilk still trapped in its body. With the boiled portions of bream, salted and peppered, washed down with Sean's delicious tea, it was feast enough to set before a king.

The evening sun settled gently behind the heathery hill of Bolus, its last rays like little rivers of gold cascading over the steep steps of the darkening cliff face, growing thinner and thinner by the second, until only faint golden threads remained before vanishing entirely. We sat there in the peaceful solitude of the eve, waiting until the first hour of darkness would elapse before hauling our pots. The only sound emerging from the muted silence was the soft murmuring ripple of water flowing gently among rock crannies within the caves. We carried a paraffin lamp with globe and wick called a hurricane lantern. This provided enough dim light to enable us to see what the pots contained when we hauled.

I sat near the bow sheeting where we stowed fishing gear of a light kind. Sean, who could not contain himself sitting idly, asked me to hand him a fishing line, which we kept coiled on square wooden frames. He could not resist the adventure of testing the unknown with a fishing line and would say: 'One never knows what's down there! You'll catch something, if it's only trouble.' He used soft crabmeat bait, which he wrapped carefully around the bright steel hook with some soft cotton yarn that he kept for that purpose. Before casting the line I saw Sean gazing upwards towards the cliff top, his countenance wearing a tense, fixed expression. He exclaimed in Gaelic: '*Dalladh is caochadh ortsa go háirithe. An bhfeiceann tú an striapach ag féachaint anuas orainn?'* ('Blinded and sightless be you without a doubt. Can you see the red whore looking down on us?') Looking upwards, I observed a large, red fox sitting on its haunches on a little knoll overlooking the cave. The fox was taboo where fishing was concerned; totally disapproved of and unmentionable. Sean felt very strongly in favour of the old superstition that a fox, a red-haired woman and fishing were a bad mix. 'Never mind,' I assured him, 'give the bait a try, at any rate!' Sean reluctantly played the line overboard until it reached the bottom. While waiting patiently for a nibble, some time passed ere Sean said: 'I feel some miserable creature down there tearing at my bait.' Suddenly he started to haul what seemed to be a very small fish, which proved to be a species of mini-wrasse, called in Gaelic *moirín*, meaning the mother of the gunner wrasse. A more abject specimen of fish is hard to imagine. It wouldn't provide a dinner for a mouse. Sean flung it back in disgust, saying: 'It will soon be time to haul our lobster pots.' Clewing up the line on its frame, he wished affliction on the baleful villain fox, which he blamed for such a poor evening's fishing.

Night having fallen, we pulled on our yellow oilskins, which protected us from the water that came aboard with the rope. We lit the lantern, which showed only its dim light. The haul was good for fifty pots. We got twenty-five lobsters of good size. At least we had thirty shillings' worth, at fifteen shillings a dozen, if the price did not slump. We were happy, but we would never be rich. The savage black conger were few and any that we caught on a wrecking rampage we lulled to sleep with the charms of the goddess Nemesis. Having replaced missing bait and reset the pots, we rowed back to the pier and stored the fish in a floating crate. We would meet again for the morning haul after a good night's rest.

The grey Atlantic seal is a very intelligent animal. Where and when a fisherman may set a net, the seal will surely find it, if it is anywhere within its territory. It has a very keen sense of hearing and of observation and is perceptive of the fisherman's movements. It can propel itself rocket-like through the water at an astonishing speed, following the fisherman far out to sea and gorging itself with the fish from his nets. Miles from land in the darkness of night, it will cram itself until it can eat no more, and always at the fisherman's expense. I have watched the herd bask on flat rocks under the midday sun. Some of the great bulls attain a ponderous weight, presenting a very unwieldy appearance on land that is so different from the acrobatic agility they display in water. We are told that the seal possesses a large brain, hence its intelligence, and it is easily trained from infancy. The seal is also very curious, becoming fascinated with music, especially that of the button accordion.

Sean believed the folklore story that seals were part of the human world at one time. One day Sean and myself were waiting at Little Skellig for our skipper, John Fitzgerald, to bring us food supplies from the mainland. We were in the rowing boat, anchored in a cave at the south side of the rock. Sean responded to a common but rather urgent call of nature. Unzipping his trousers, he eased his tail clear of the stern transom, enjoying with relief and satisfaction the smooth flow of events, when suddenly out of the blue ocean came a great, splattering splash, sprinkling and dousing Sean's back porch with water, accompanied by a loud exploding 'poofh!' of exhaling air. Sean jumped in terror into the stern sheeting, struggling with his trousers, which had fallen about his ankles. Looking behind him, he saw that a large grey seal was staring at us, his head and shoulders exposed within a half a metre of the transom. Giving another loud 'poofh!' he dived beneath the surface, and Sean exclaimed in Gaelic: '*Gurab é do tharrac deirneach é, a bhastaird!*' ('That it may be your last breath, you bastard!') Later on we both laughed heartily at what seemed like a human prank.

Sean has now passed on. He was a good neighbour, with a knowledge of Gaelic from his cradle days, and a great conversationalist with a broad sense of humour who loved the art of storytelling. Not one word of English did he ever use while in conversation with me, but the purest of Gaelic. If there is one tribute I can pay to my comrade fisherman and complete Gael, it will be in the words of Shakespeare: 'Good night, sweet prince, / And flights of angels sing thee to thy rest.'

South Wind

A wind speaks
From the south tonight,
Whispering
'My windowpane,
I am the breath you breathe
To live,
Born when planets spun.

'Long ere the frame of man
Was formed,
I helped the seas to fill.
I am the life
Of the peat-pyre flame.
The fisherman
Home from the wave
And the bogman
Home from the hill,

'Together they watch
Aged seasons burn,
Pictures of million
Aeons unturn.
Bog-cotton
Whitens the heather again.
And beetle boatmen
Stroke a peat-pond main
Where dart
Of damsel dragon
And honey bees sip

The mottled lip
Of orchid and ragged robin.

'The fisherman home from the bay
Tends to his torn mesh.
The bogman from the heath
Piles peat-pyre upon the hearth.'

'PLEASE, MISTER, HOLD MY BABY ...'

Johnny Sullivan was a broad-shouldered, squat man with thick arms and a hairy barrel-chest always open to the elements. He maintained that the torso was an extension of the face and should not be covered or muffled. He scorned the term catching cold; 'God's leather to God's weather' was his maxim. He walked on land as he would on the deck of a rolling ship. His legs seemed to hang loosely from the sinews of his knees. Some of the harbour loafers would remark as he went by: 'Heavy ground swell' or 'She's rolling bad today, Johnny.' His broad, dark features, the tuft of black beard on the point of his chin, and the black peaked yachting cap on his crown made him look more like a Breton sea-captain than an Irishman. He was nicknamed Johnny the Crab. He had the drowning man's grip, what was termed in Gaelic *greim an duine bháite*, on anything he decided he must hold on to.

Johnny came of good Irish ancestry. His grandfather, Paddy John Tom, was evicted on two occasions during the campaign of the Land League. For obstructing a bailiff on the day of the eviction, he earned a two-month incarceration in the gaol in lovely Tralee town, whose infamous history is indelibly enshrined in the folk tales, songs and stories of County Kerry.

Paddy John Tom was about to be evicted for a third time, only to gain a reprieve on compassionate grounds and on the word of an understanding sheriff. The day before the eviction was to take place, Paddy had sought the advice of John Roche, his neighbour, who was known to one and all as the wise man of the neighbourhood and also well known for his ability to formulate plans. He had a genius for invention and resourcefulness. Paddy John knew he was on his last chance to hold on to his farm in Carraig. Only through the good influence of Father Brown had he been reinstated on two occasions previously.

John Roche advised him that he must feign mental derangement when the sheriff would arrive tomorrow. He was to present himself entirely in the nude, his hair dishevelled, doing a grotesque dance, and he must begrime his body with cow manure and filth to look as loathsome as possible. He was to welcome the sheriff and his officers by speaking some incoherent gibberish. His wife and children were to appear distraught, imploring the sheriff to send them a doctor.

Paddy John Tom acted the moon calf with such skill that next morning that some of the neighbours who had gathered to witness the eviction were moved to tears. The grand priest, Father Brown, who came in haste to the scene was taken aback, declaring in a husky voice: 'I never thought I'd see the day that Paddy John Tom would crack up like that!' The sheriff signed a paper giving Paddy a respite for another quarter-year, which he gave to the good priest, saying: 'I think he needs medical attention, Father, and after that and most importantly, some money to clear his rent arrears. This is his last warning.' The sheriff and his officers then departed.

The upshot of the matter was that Paddy John Tom made a remarkable recovery after washing the cow dung off his skin in the pool under the old bridge.

Father Brown was told in confidence that the doctor was not needed, that the shock of the cold water would restore his mental faculties.

Not long after, Paddy was heir to the legacy of a brother who had died in Montana. This enabled him to keep the old homestead at Carraig and to pay off all outstanding arrears. And so the farm remained in Paddy's family, right up to Johnny the Crab's time. Johnny's tribe, the Sullivans, were related by marriage to our family somewhere in the unwritten past, long before shotgun weddings or letters of freedom were invented. Maybe it was a Diarmuid and Gráinne-style wedlock that linked our clans. Maybe it was a bed on some hillside, with the most natural result transpiring, that led to a woman of the Ua Ciarmhaic clan becoming the mother of a Sullivan.

At any rate, Johnny, who was much praised for his faultless rendering of the 'Rocks of Bawn', boasted that his vocal vibrations were due to contact with an Ua Ciarmhaic woman who, according to local lore, was a bird of the nightingale family. Never cut out to be a farmer, he took a berth on a boat that fished for mackerel out of Ballinskelligs, taking to the water like a young otter. He spent many years on various boats learning different skills. He excelled at mending and mounting all types of fishing nets and making and sewing sails. I could watch him knitting new meshes into a damaged net forever. The wooden needle loaded with twine flashed in and out with a wondrous sleight and dexterity. He was indeed a master of his trade.

Johnny tried courtship with an English girl, a beautiful Saxon blonde whose father, Paul Crampton, was in ill health. A retired ship's captain, he owned a small house on the far side of the bay. Johnny became his right-hand man and before long they were fast friends, enjoying many fishing trips together. Johnny became engaged to Gloria and when Paul Crampton passed away he moved in with his bride-to-be. The expected marital bliss never materialized. Gloria was wild as a March hare. She danced, drank, frolicked and flirted to excess, and in a short time she secretly sold the house and hightailed it to England.

The sudden crisis in Johnny's life left him crestfallen and disconsolate. All thoughts of Gloria and her beguiling, cheating trickery became unbearable. In a mood of low-spirited melancholy he decided he must change his lifestyle and try his luck in England. The year being 1913, he took passage from Cork on a schooner that ran general cargo from London for a Cork city firm. Now Johnny relates his own story, a tale that turns out to be so unlikely as to be incredible to his family and friends, had it not come from his own lips:

'Captain Paddy Kearns was a Kerryman and skipper of the *Mary Rose* and, being a friend of my father's, he gave me free passage to London. In return I helped with working the ship. The voyage was short and successful, helped by a smart north breeze. We berthed at a company warehouse in the port of London in four days and some hours. I had the magnificent sum of twelve pounds in my purse, which I had saved from the autumn herring season the year previously. Would to God that I had stayed with fishing rather than take the leap of a sheep into the abyss!

'I had an aunt, Brigid Sullivan, who kept a boarding house in Kilburn, and I had her address written on an envelope, which I kept like a holy relic. It was the only link with home, and it gave me hope of survival in London after I said goodbye to kind Captain Kearns of the *Mary Rose*. I asked my way to the Kilburn district of a dockland policeman who plied me with questions and particulars relating to my identity. When finished he said: "Look here, Paddy, your best bet is to hire a cabby and cabs is cheap, mate.' In fact he was very helpful. He called a cab, the driver of which spoke with a short, cockney accent that I was to hear more of later. "Where to, Irish?" I gave him the address, 17 Highbury Lane, Kilburn, to which he replied: "Get on board, mate." The trip to Kilburn was short and the cockney's fee was half a crown. I gave him an extra shilling, which he acknowledged with "Decent bloke."

'Aunt Brigid was surprised to see me. She said I had hit London at the wrong time, that work was scarce. Her clients were all long-term boarders and she didn't have an extra bedroom but I was welcome to sleep on a settle bed in the back kitchen until I got suitable digs. Hobson's choice! Oh, for the loft of my father's cowbyre and a bed of last summer's fragrant hay, the warm air from the breathing cows beneath, their bedding transferring the heat from their bodies upwards. I envied those cattle their warm stalls in Carraig in preference to a settle bed in a back kitchen in Kilburn on a frosty morning in February. My aunt asked: "Did you feel the cold last night, Johnny? I think you might need an extra blanket."

' "Think I might need!" I felt like telling her. But silence is golden. My teeth chattered and my skin raised goose pimples with stems like mushrooms. Some nights I envied Sam Magee and wished I'd been stuffed into the furnace beside him. All the raunchy rhymes I ever heard seemed to haunt me in a succession of cold shivers: "As cold as a frog in an icy pool, / As cold as the tip of an Eskimo's tool."

'One of my aunt's boarders was a man called Amos de Malo, a gentle and concerned person. He had charge of the heating system in a large London store. It was he who found part-time work for me in the loading department. Any job was better than none, I thought, until I knew my way around. I was to meet Amos outside the main shopping centre at two o'clock sharp. He was to get me acquainted with my new boss in the loading department. To make sure I would be on time, I arrived fifteen minutes early. Not more than five minutes had elapsed when a gorgeous-looking female who was holding a beautiful baby in her arms approached me. Walking smartly up to me, she thrust the baby into my arms saying: "Please, Mister, hold my baby and my suitcase, it is urgent that I call a taxi at once. It will only take a minute."

'The telephone kiosk stood only a dozen yards away. I watched her enter. In the meantime I glanced at the beautiful blue eyes of the child I held gingerly, who was dressed in snow-white garments with a beautiful short coat of grey fur and hood to match. I looked towards the phone booth once more and to my consternation the gorgeous female had vanished. At that moment Big Ben struck two o'clock.

'True to his word, Amos arrived on the stroke. He had naturally bulging eyes and the suggestion of an impish grin very near the surface, as if a pent-up volcano of laughter was about to explode. Now his eyes bulged more than usual; any fool could see that.

' "Johnny," he ventured, "don't tell me you have been left holding the baby. If the lady don't show up soon you'd better call the cops. I must report for work. Sorry Johnny! See you soon, I hope."

'The stark reality set in. I stood there dumbfounded, waiting in vain for some woman, mother or other, to return. I cursed all the women I ever knew. It was because of Gloria Crampton's treachery that I had left home in the first place, only now to be gulled once more by some guileful girl the moment I set foot in England. I nearly screamed aloud. I hate the sneaky bitches. Why me? I'll dump the child. A voice within me seemed to say, hold on, Johnny, you came from a woman too. Would you condemn your own mother because you came from her womb? Rubbish! This was not the time for me to tease out some unreasonable philosophy. I was not a coward but I felt some winged creatures flutter in my stomach.

'At this stage the child wailed piteously. People stopped and stared as I beckoned to two policemen who were already walking towards me. They listened sympathetically, I thought, or at least they gave me that impression. Things seemed to be going my way until I mentioned that the lady also left a suitcase in my care. They immediately said: "We must see what it contains."

' "It's over here," I said.

'The suitcase was left only a dozen yards away from the place where I was standing. We retraced our steps but to my horror the case had vanished. I tried to explain: "But it was here a minute ago," I blurted.

'One of the bobbies said: "Save your wind, Paddy! You've got to do better than that."

'One policeman departed, while the other said: "Take it easy, mate. It's only routine, but you must come to the station."

'I said: "Why not take the baby? I haven't done anything wrong."

' "Yes, Irish, that may be so, a man is innocent until proven guilty."

'I still argued that the woman had worn a most expensive fur coat.

' "Paddy, in London or Paris well dressed could mean fur coat and no knickers."

'At last the light was beginning to dawn. Back home in Carraig girls only wore black shawls. Alas, poor Gubbins the Gawk! A Black Maria arrived out of nowhere. I was ushered inside, baby and all. If Captain Kearns of the *Mary Rose* saw me now, what salty expressions would he use – not what the Church would call prayers, surely. The authorities that upheld the unsullied pillars of society were sharing at least part of my pickle.

'I had never changed a nappy in my life but the smell seemed to urgently demand such an operation and it was becoming more pronounced. We arrived at the police station where I was questioned by the desk sergeant, a huge man with a florid complexion and a black walrus-type moustache, the extreme last hairs of which extended to the lobes of his ears and were waxed to a needle-point. His pot belly would eventually eclipse his trouser belt, and the buttons of his fly seemed under severe intestinal pressure, ready to burst open at any moment. Giving an oblique glance in my direction, he proceeded to ask questions: my address in Ireland, nationality, religion, occupation and so on. All went well until he asked me the name of the baby.

' "I do not know!"

' "Male or female?"

' "I do not know!"

' "You do not know whether your baby is male or female?"

'At this point I was beginning to lose my cool.

' "I have already told you all I know about the baby

and its supposed mother. The baby is not mine and if you want to know whether it is male or female, why not call a doctor and have it examined?"

'Walrus Whiskers insisted that I answer his questions and kept covering the same ground until I wasn't sure of my answers anymore. The other PC stood at my side like the proverbial pillar of salt. At last he read the list of questions and answers for my benefit and asked me to sign. What a relief that was! It was the first time in two hours that I had the chance to lay the baby down from my arms. I placed the little bundle carefully on the desk, near the dossier I was about to sign. When I had finished the signature, the burly desk sergeant said: "Pick up your baby, Paddy." At this point I decided I must make a protest. I remained silent and immobile. He repeated the order and asked if I was disobeying him. I answered by telling him that in my opinion the baby needed attention and that I was unqualified to cater for its welfare. Walrus Whiskers' blood pressure soared, if his purple complexion was anything to go by. Suddenly, he grabbed the telephone and spoke some curt jargon I failed to understand. In the meantime, the other two policemen went into a huddle and then made a prolonged phone call while Walrus glowered in my direction.

'The door of the room opened to two high-ranking officers followed by a jovial-faced, buxom matron in nurses uniform, who immediately took the neglected baby gently in her arms and left the room. One of the officers, a chief constable, said: "Owing to the fact that we can't establish any criminal charge against you or disprove your story, it is our duty to procure an order placing you and the baby in protective custody. No doubt you will help us with any further evidence."

'The chief constable was very courteous. He asked

for the name of the RIC sergeant in my district in Ireland and for the name of the vicar or parish priest and my own relations, answers that would help in establishing my identity.

' "For the present, and until proven otherwise, we must regard the baby as your property. We will provide accommodation for you and the child in a welfare institution – a home for abandoned children, unmarried mothers and rape pregnancies. And men in similar circumstances."

'My heart plunged to my toes. Why do I not mention my Aunt Brigid or Amos de Malo? They could vouch for my identity. No, no, I must not get them involved in this stupid mess, I reasoned silently.

'My reverie ended there.

' "Come, John, you will accompany the officer and the nurse to the welfare centre."

'The Black Maria sped through the streets once more before arriving at the institution, a large building with lifts, stairways, playrooms, dining halls, sleeping cubicles and a prison-like atmosphere. The place smelled of disinfectant and everyone wore blue-and-white uniforms. The gates swung shut, clanging like a funeral bell.

'I was led into an office where the matron was seated in a private section from which she could observe all. The officer presented her with the file, signed a document and departed. The baby's arm was marked with some kind of rubber stamp, for identification I presumed. Turning to me, she said: "You are a special category person. You will perform light duties during your stay. Our code of discipline must be observed at all times. You will hand up your clothing and other valuables for which you will be given a signed receipt. You will be allowed to care for your baby for two hours per day and shown how to change and feed your child under strict professional supervision. There is no smoking or alcohol allowed. There is a recreation and reading room."

'The attendant escorted me down the corridor to my cubicle, which was nine feet square. The bed was without a headboard but had a rough mattress, two grey cotton sheets, two grey blankets and a bottle-shaped pillow. Toilets and washrooms were central. The attendant provided a cardboard box for my clothes. I got a set of underwear and overalls with the logo of the institution on the garments. I felt like I was part of a penal settlement. The lines of an old Fenian ballad seemed to torment my addled brain. I felt like singing aloud:

> Convict garb and the broad arrow,
> His proud soul could never harrow,
> A rebel to the very marrow.

'All for the sake of an unwanted child! What kind of mother would trust her child to a stranger? I was no different. I too wanted to get rid of the baby as quickly as possible. Alas! Poor innocent child, you are nobody's baby, I thought. Perhaps I was beginning to let some of the guilt rub off on myself. I felt a little confused. Having changed into my new, ill-fitting gear, I was shown to the dining hall. The food was wholesome: beef stew, vegetables and plenty of potatoes. I slurped it down ravenously, being very hungry. Some inmates sniggered at my uncouth table manners, and purposely, to make matters worse, I made belching noises and wiped my lips with the back of my hand. One venturesome chap tried to strike up a conversation by asking questions that were not to my liking. Another jostled me in the corridor. Having failed once he tried a second time, only to receive a floating elbow midship. That caused the horseplay to end abruptly. The aspiring bully lost his appetite.

'Breakfast was at 6 am sharp. The first gong for rising went at 5.30 am. Then you washed and shaved, folded your bedclothes and swept your room. This was like navy routine: heave out, lash up and stow. My first baptism of "light work" entailed scrubbing a section of floor, twenty feet by twenty. No mops with long handles. Oh, no! That was not what scrubbing floors meant. Down on your hands and knees was the order, like old Jack Tar in the days of Nelson. I had to "holy-stone the deck and scrape the cable".

'My first social contact with unmarried mothers in captivity was on my second day when a portly female officer of Amazonian physique introduced me to the female scrubbing section. She was of battle-clad, iron-side proportions. I would not dream of having a naval engagement with her, let alone fire a shot across her bows. She presented me with a pail half-filled with luke-warm water, a coarse scrubbing brush, some soap and a sponge. Indicating the territory wherein I must work, the stewardess departed. I muttered some unprintable, self-reproachful words to myself, got down on my knees and started to scrub. Young girls to the right of me, grown women to the left of me, as busy as beavers scrubbing the place clean. One teenager whispered: "Don't use too much soap, just scrub and wipe. Why are you here? Have you a baby for the orphanage?"

'She was a sweet young girl serving her time. She had had her baby three months earlier in the institution's hospital and was to be allowed to leave in a few days. She asked me if I could help her with even a little money. Much as I needed it myself, I felt I could not refuse, so I slipped her a pound note when no one was looking. I could see her face light up. She made a surprising remark: "Thank you. I'll pray for you."

'It was the first time I had heard the word prayer since leaving home and certainly I did not have recourse to prayer in my present situation. The girl had her own troubles, but she still believed in prayer. Taken aback, I blurted out: "God bless you!"

'She answered: "This is a cold, bleak place."

'I couldn't remember when anyone called God's blessing on me. I felt depressed. The whole atmosphere of the institution seemed to close in on me. It was at this juncture that an attendant called my name, telling me to report to the office at once. I was taken before the matron. She took an official form from a file, and asked me to attach my signature, saying: "You have now signed your discharge papers, which I witnessed and date-stamped. Now go to your cubicle where you will find your clothing and personal belongings. You are to be released unconditionally by order of the police department, who found the mother and the missing suitcase."

'They had a taxi waiting to take me to 17 Highbury Lane. My Aunt Brigid and Amos had contacted the police in Kilburn and helped to establish my innocence. I asked if I could see the baby before I departed. The matron smiled and said curtly: "The baby is no longer your responsibility. You have been saved a lot of hassle, thanks to our efficient police force. The taxi is waiting, Mr Sullivan, you must leave now."

'Just like that: cold, methodical and stiff, like the institution. But I was fortunate. I had tasted a mere morsel from the bread of incarceration. I remembered lines from a poem in my schoolbook: "I'm free! I am free! I'll return no more, / My weary time in this cage is over." What a wonderful word is freedom; personal liberty from slavery, serfdom, confinement and bondage.

> Oh! Had I the wings of a bird,
> To soar through the blue sunny sky,
> By what breeze would my pinions be stirred?
> To what beautiful land would I fly?

'I got a wonderful welcome from Aunt Brigid and Amos de Malo. I'd nearly have ventured another flight, there was so much joy in returning. I had so many questions to answer; the story was so ridiculously bizarre. It could only be a once-off and, of course, could only happen to Gubbins the Gawk.

'My intended job had been filled and I was not disappointed. By now I tended to think that city life had certain restrictions incompatible with my upbringing. I told my aunt that it was my intention to return to Ireland again. She agreed that it was probably the right decision. Rumour was spreading that the emperor Kaiser Wilhelm was preparing for war. How true were those reports! Many thousands were to perish soon in the mud of Flanders, in the most wretched conditions, leaving behind grisly monuments called war memorials. So much for the empire builders.

'The *Mary Rose* made monthly trips to the port of London. It was now the month of March. I looked up the list of arrivals and departures published in the shipping report and there, right enough, was listed her name, arriving at the port of London from Cork, Ireland, on 14 March. I was thrilled with the thought of escaping from the maw of this great city. The grand streets and avenues, alas, only cover the rotten stinking sewers beneath, where so much human heartbreak, sorrow, remorse and misery go unnoticed. On the other

Skelligs Sunset

hand, caught up in the web was the beautiful young girl in the orphanage who was brave enough to have recourse to prayer. I rebuked myself for not accepting the challenge of London. Maybe it was cowardly of me, but the clear seas around Ireland were calling me again.

'The days went by quickly. I visited the dockland in the company of Amos, where we spoke with stevedores who informed us that the *Mary Rose* was berthed upstream at warehouse number nine. Further information was given on receipt of half a crown. The various captains could be found in a dockside tavern called The Sailor's Joy, a famous place that catered for emotional excitement or for those who indulged in the rites and orgiastic revelry of Dionysus and Bacchus.

'Having taken a taxi to the port the following day, I met Captain Kearns and renewed our friendship over a drink in The Sailor's Joy. He was worried about the talk on everyone's lips of impending war. He was to sail to Ireland on the twentieth, and I came on board the morning before. Aunt Brigid and Amos came to see me off. She gave me a gift of ten pounds, which was a fortune in itself, on the promise that I ask my father to find a house for her in Ireland. Amos gave me a packet tied with blue silk ribbon that was not to be opened until I reached Ireland. The gift was a beautiful baby blue-eyed doll, dressed in a white fur jacket – now one of my treasured possessions.

'The voyage back to Ireland was uneventful. Having rounded the Scillies, it was a straight run for the Tuskar. The *Mary Rose* ran before a favourable sailing wind, carrying a bone in her teeth all the way to Roche's Point, where we anchored for the night. On deck, I could smell the fragrance of rural Ireland borne on the land breeze. It was good to be back again!

168

'Please, Mister, Hold My Baby ...'

And doesn't old Cobh,
Look charming there,
Watching the wild waves motion,
Leaning her back against the hills,
With the tips of her toes in the ocean.'

Storm Petrel

They name you
Mother Carey's chick,
Abandoned waif
Of storm.
Why your raucous,
Mocking chuckle,
Web-toed, witching wisp,
Surf-boarding the seething,
Tumbling lip
Of curling frothing billow?
O happy creature
Who can sleep
Contentedly
In far-flung heaving
Pastures deep
Which make
Your bedtime pillow!
Before Columbus
Ere set sail
You wave-danced storms –
Yes, long before
Flying Dutchman's wraith
Did haunt
Stout mariners who dared
With broken spar
And torn sail
To battle
With the scourging wave
Of mighty Horn.

Mysterious sprite,
Are you the David
Of the deep
Who watched proud
Goliath-galleons
Sink to sleep?
What balance
In wild nature's house
You keep!
New sailors do not
Fear you any more!
Sea witch,
It's cradle time
Once more!
New joy,
New chicks,
New love nests
On the shore.

HUMPTY-DUMPTY

Man is prone to malady. We hear of prehistoric man described by anthropologists who call their findings, 'the phenomenon of man', Peking man, Neanderthal man and caveman, who were letting us know they were hunters and artists by carvings and engravings left in underground caverns. The anthropologists seem so sure; they even tell us that this phenomenal person ate wild dogs. Of course he did! The greedy little fellow was already commercially inclined. The Americans and the Germans caught on to it immediately, leaving us the hot dog trade and the bow-wow sausage, still best-sellers to this day.

One thing they never tell us: that this distant relation of ours must have taken a hell of a chance when he ate his first blackberry. No wonder they kicked him out of the Garden. Some chancer! Because of him we have all been trying to claw our way back ever since. So who was blamed for it all? Poor Mother Eve, of course. Was it she who offered him that first blackberry? I am led to believe that God created man in the image of His own likeness. What happened before or after the Fall is entirely beyond my comprehension. All I know is that man holds the status of being the most educated, superior animal who governs the earth and is possibly about to take the place of the greatest Humpty-Dumpty of all time.

I have described myself as a victim prone to malaise. Have you, Humpty-Dumpty, experienced a bout of seasickness, *breoiteacht farraige* in Gaelic? I'll venture *mal de mer* in French. It is a general feeling of discomfort brought about by the swaying motion of a boat, a most nauseating experience. At its best you want to vomit your guts out and at its worst the empty, retching strain will make your anus protrude, which might need medical attention. In the Irish dictionary the anus is described as the posterior opening of the alimentary canal, *poll na tóna*, meaning just a plain arsehole. The Irish peasant (speaking only for myself) had another word for the lower bowel, *bundún. Chuir sé a bhundún amach.* He simply put out his *bundún.*

I suffered my first and only bout of seasickness in a small rowing boat while searching for wreckage during the First World War. The bay had a high but not dangerous groundswell. After consigning my breakfast to Davy Jones, I lay on the bow sheeting and slept, thus ending my initiation. Never again, thankfully, did I suffer from *breoiteacht farraige.*

One great sea fisherman I can vouch for who was plagued by seasickness and could not afford to relinquish his livelihood, experienced a spasm so severe he knew that what he disgorged was somewhat unreal: a jelly-like mass of small egg yolks. Some, he swore, were green, blue, pale yellow and bloody. In medical terms must have been some form of bile. From that day onwards he enjoyed good health as a fisherman and lived to a fine old age.

During my time as a fisherman I observed the different and various forms of seasickness and the horrible sinking feeling some martyrs recounted. A female friend of mine who had occasion to travel to England during the First World War was so sick that she said it would be the kindest act the Germans ever did if they would only sink the bloody ship.

During the Irish College terms in Ballinskelligs, sixty or more years ago, we fishermen were asked to take the students on boat trips to Skellig Michael. On one such day several students became sick. Standing in line at the side of the boat, they started to puke with prolonged persistence. Standing among the younger group I observed an older man who turned out to be a teacher. He was really under the weather, between spewing, groaning, muttering and intermittent explosions of superfluous gas from his exhaust. I took him to be in dire need of compassion. Laying my hand on his shoulder I said: 'You seem very weak, sir! Is there any way I can help you? Perhaps a drop of brandy or something?' Boy, was I taken aback! He turned on me with a scowling, audacious look and uttered an expletive that only deep seamen use: 'What do you mean man? Me, weak? Can't you see I'm pitching it as far as the rest of them!' Later on we landed on the Rock and all had some rest and refreshments. The return trip was not so bad except that one girl had immersed her hands and wrists under water as a cure, only to find that her gold wristwatch was not waterproof. Another passenger consigned some dentures to the sea in an explosive contraction.

My father was a great believer in small boats of eighteen to twenty feet in length. He would say: 'Big ships flounder and small boats float.' Survival at sea to him meant many things: reading the sky at dawn for the coming day and reading the evening sky for the morrow; the study of sea currents that seem unusual; a sudden change of wind; such small signs as cat's-paws; patches of calm; little whirlwinds like mini tornadoes or the strange behaviour of birds entering or leaving the bay, especially the gannet and the many gull and diving species he was familiar with since boyhood. He knew he must learn from wild, unexpected whims of his environment that might suddenly threaten his survival. He was keen to impart this information to his offspring. He taught me how to eat raw shrimp, which were health-giving and tasty. I really developed a liking for raw scallop, which we seldom got. If a lobster shed a claw he would carefully remove the shell and give us portions to chew. Raw lobster is sweet and palatable. Even the raw limpet is full of nourishment. Just cut off his horns and pull out his little tiny gut string, pop him in your mouth, simply chew and Bob's your uncle. My father was not asking us to become Robinson Crusoes, only teaching a simple lesson – that it is possible to survive for an indefinite period at sea without fancy food. And I do not have to teach you how to catch rainwater in an Irish climate: just open your mouth and look up at the sky.

On the other side of the coin, a fisherman is prone to an ailment similar to seasickness described by some seamen as 'a real shit of a hangover'. In less vulgar circles it would be described in more elegant language as a scatological encounter. Some would boast they drink Canada Dry and Russian vodka for chasers. One of my companions was threatened with gall-bladder trouble. On seeking medical advice he said the good doctor told him to keep his gallstones swimming in porter and he would be okay, which counsel he prudently and strictly adhered to. He often sang a little ditty. Maybe he was being humorously critical of himself, lifting his glass he would say:

> My first pint swallowed,
> A second soon will follow,

Third, fourth and fifth
Make ribald mirth
Sound hollow.
Woe, dark glass!
Thou venom-frothed tool
That saps the sense
And makes a wise man fool.

Only a drop of raw spirits would settle the sinking sickness of a beautiful vomiting hangover, according to the wisdom of an old Gaelic quatrain:

Cuirse chughat más fonn leat
Teacht id' shláinte
Ruibe de chlúmh'
Na gcú san lá arna mháireach.

Take a hair of the dog
That bit you
And do not live
In sorrow
If you wish
Good health tomorrow.

What I learned from my parents as a boy in my teens now seems to be all old hat. New technology proves that man is becoming exceedingly clever. Whither goest thou, Homo sapiens? Who called me wise? Am I only attempting to appear wise? I am not acting the ape any more. We have plumbed the depths of the ocean and conquered the air in flight, satellites flitting around able to tell us our way in the dark. We are ready to build dust-flats on the moon and a Mars Bar factory on the red planet, yet we have not discovered how a cow manufactures milk from green grass!

Mike, Jack, Con and Florrie. All of them, except myself, are now deceased.

Before starting our first workday we were assembled in classroom order in the shed, which served as the professor's office and that of the students. Bespectacled, he sat behind his desk and lectured us on how he expected us to behave during the period of excavation. We stood meekly, cap in hand, all except Florrie who still wore his cap at an alarmingly acute angle. I always expected it to become disengaged, but somehow it still clung there. Flor wore it too well; to see him decapped would be like seeing a bishop without his mitre.

The professor spoke to us at length about the people who had supposedly built this wedge-shaped tomb of the early Bronze Age; mysterious people who were the first settlers in Ireland. Describing the expected finds, he said: 'We may find pieces of honey-coloured flint, tiny arrow heads, perhaps shards of red, thin pottery or an urn, beaker-shaped, which always, whenever found, stands mouth downwards, under which might be fragments of human charred bone or ash. For want of a better name, we could call their owners "Beaker People" and evidence would suggest that they voyaged from the shores of Brittany four thousand years ago.'

When it rained we were not allowed to come within the wooden tool-shed and we were told that we could build our own improvised shelter with sods of clay, which leaked incessantly like a sieve. We were also told bluntly not to answer any questions put to us by any visitors or newspaper men, because we were not qualified to speak about our work to anyone in the outside world. I suddenly realized that the old adage was brutally true: Officers do not drink with the men.

My Ship Sailed Without Me

My ship sailed without me
This morning,
Out on the dawning tide,
Her soft sails swelling,
Blue waters
Cleaving from her side.

Gliding, ever gliding,
Away on the ebbing stream,
Dipping the far horizon,
Vanish my cherished dreams.

Cold are the mists of dockland,
Enshrouding this heart of mine.
Leaving me here, my tall ship,
Reaching for the line.

DAN OF THE ROADS

I only knew him as Dan; he never divulged his full name to me, though we became fast friends. He was a man of the roads, the roadways of Ireland. He knew them all, every bend and turn, hill and hollow, and most of all, I think, he had explored as a wayfarer the dusty road of life itself. I was living alone at the time when I first met him. It was a dreary night in the autumn. I had just come back from a fishing trip that a howling gale had forced us to abandon. It was late at night. The rain fell in wind-blown fury. As I was inserting the key in the lock of my darkened cottage door, a voice from the nearby cow-byre startled me.

'It's a bad night, sir!'

I turned the key in the lock, pushed the door open, struck a match and lit the oil-lamp before answering. Going back to the door, I called out: 'Yes, it's a bad night. If you need shelter come in.'

I stood away from the light. I was not going to be taken unawares by a voice from the darkness. I heard heavy footsteps coming across the yard towards the house. Then he appeared: a burly, bearded figure framed in the doorway, water dripping from a battered felt hat that covered his ears and the collar of his shabby black overcoat. Standing still, he exclaimed abruptly: 'God bless all here, sir. My name is Dan. Will you give me shelter from the storm, sir?'

'Yes,' I said, 'Come in and get rid of your wet clothing.'

I heard him mutter for the first time a blessing that I was to hear a thousand more times from his lips: 'May God and His Holy Mother bless you, sir.'

Later on when we got to know each other better, I told him where to find the key in a secret hiding place if I was away from home. He never once used it to his advantage. He would sleep in the hedge first. He could converse on any subject. He had the most incredible tales and he enjoyed telling them. He loved card games, but hated swearing. He enjoyed smoking a pipe, and went to great pains to prepare for a full, enjoyable smoke. He kept a special knitting pin in a flat tin case to keep the pipe-stem free from nicotine tar. He would clean the bowl of the pipe of all ash and shred the tobacco until it was as fine as wool. Finally, he would add a little rum mixed with honey to moisten the shredded tobacco. The rum-and-honey mixture he kept in a small bottle. Sometimes he would include a little piece of cedar wood to give the smoke an aroma. When filling his pipe he made sure the task was done properly by placing a little morsel of tobacco in the bottom of the bowl, then a little circular piece as thin as a cent, never pressing downwards, but rather towards the side wall of the pipe, and then placing a pad of tobacco on the surface. The pipe was lit evenly, and left to quench before finally being lit again for an enjoyable smoke. I often proffered him a cigarette. He never refused, but said: 'Sure that's not smoking at all, sir!'

During the war years there was an occasion when his pedlar's licence was out of date. The licence was obtainable at a nominal sum. He would not risk peddling or be seen in public until it was renewed. He had developed an ingrained fear of authority that was perhaps congenital, maybe a throwback to the penal laws. 'A policeman must do his duty. He has sworn an oath, sir,' he would say. I would bring his tobacco supply. He wanted only the best: sliced plug tobacco that was sold in tins. I kept a supply handy, in case he would arrive unexpectedly out of nowhere. I could immediately sense when he was short of the weed. His otherwise cheerful demeanour would seem overcast with an air of gloom, but his face would light up in a childlike smile on being told that I had a supply waiting for him. He would always mutter half to himself: 'May God and His Holy Mother bless you, sir.'

Once his licence was renewed, he was off on the road again, carrying a bag resembling a haversack flat between his shoulders, over that a satchel and a shoulder bag, two side bags of light, black leather, and an extra canvas bag in the crook of his arm. In his right hand he always carried a stout blackthorn stick. 'I have never used it,' he said. 'The bold dogs have great respect for an Irish blackthorn.' As the years passed, Dan developed a stooping, headlong gait, as if hurrying to reach some mysterious destination. It was always the same, he was always in a hurry, except when he came to stay with me, and that was never for longer than a day at a time. He would overhaul all his merchandise, putting the different commodities each in their own satchels, cards of safety-pins, large and medium packets of needles, assorted knitting pins, thimbles, reels of sewing thread, hairpins, cards of buttons, collar studs, boot polish, sticking plaster and tin whistles, little bottles of castor oil, bootlaces, hanks of fishing line and hooks, little penknives and maybe a German scissors; all lightweight but necessary goods for the housewife. At Christmas time he sold holly, *Old Moore's Almanac*, light decoration, packs of playing cards and even cheap spectacles. Dan was the hawker supreme. He was never known to look for alms. His clothing was old-fashioned, sometimes tattered, but clean. He would collect pennies at race meetings or on a pattern day. When evening came he would summon all the children he could find to stand in a group in front of him and throw all the pennies up in fistfuls between them. Watching them scramble for the money gave him such delight that the tears would stream down his cheeks with laughter.

Dan never discussed or exchanged views on topics, local or otherwise. He was not a news-agent or a tale-bearer, therefore he hardly ever answered questions except with his usual: 'I wouldn't know, sir.' Only in winter would he seek shelter indoors. He loved sleeping by the side of a stream or under a hedge in summertime. He carried a blackened old billycan with a hinged cover in which he boiled water for his tea. He liked strong tea – very strong – and he never drank my tea. He protested that it was too watery. His tea, which he relished to the last drop, always left a heavy brown stain in the teacup.

In his declining years he came less often and unexpectedly from his long wanderings. I remember, when the Second World War broke out, he told me how it would end. How prophetic were his words: 'Hitler will die a very lonely death, forsaken by all his friends. His defeat will be so overwhelming he will die alone.' By this time Dan had given up the commercial business of peddling and passed the time playing a game like clock-patience, which he devised himself. When overcome by a sudden urge to play this game, it seemed he must get down to it. If conditions were dry, you could find him sitting on the main highway, legs crossed like a tailor, his old-fashioned hat beside him, oblivious to the world and to passing traffic, his mind so closely focused on the cards spread on the roadway.

I had reason to believe that he was a very devout person. He often said the rosary at country wakes of people whom he never could have known; and I think he exacted a penance on himself, which I only witnessed by chance. On one of the nights he stayed with me, a very frosty period in wintertime, I was awakened late at night by a moaning sound that seemed to emanate from a position outside the house. Getting out of bed to investigate, I found the kitchen door ajar and Dan's bed empty. Going outside as noiselessly as possible I beheld Dan. with arms outstretched, lying stark naked on the icy concrete footpath. Standing over him I said: 'Dan, what's the matter? Are you ill? Have you fallen?' He immediately arose and said he was sorry for having disturbed me and went back to bed, having made his apology. I did not pursue the incident any further.

Old Dan has passed on and his place in our so-called society is empty. Dan had no vanity. Perhaps at some stage he had scorned riches, but he was never a begrudger. He could laugh and crack a joke in the midst of distress, like he did on the day that he was caught in the near-hurricane winds of an October storm. I watched from my window a frail figure of humanity being buffeted like a ship without a rudder, sometimes spun around and sometimes bent double, only rising again and battling the last few steps to the door that I held open to receive him. Sitting on a chair in the middle of the kitchen floor, water streamed from his clothing. I requested him to remove his wet jacket, which he was reluctant to do. When he did, to my amazement I saw that he had no shirt or underwear beneath.

'Your shirt, Dan!' I said. 'Have you got any shirt? You'll catch your death of cold!'

Dan laughed loud and hearty. Opening his haversack, he took out his shirt and underwear, which were quite dry, saying: 'I saw the storm coming, sir. You must prepare for the rainy day.'

Dan lived a free and full life. He was a happy and peaceful person. Whatever his convictions about life or his philosophy, he kept them to himself and always gave his blessing freely: 'May God and His Holy Mother bless you, sir.'

Why the Storm?

We were only
A ripple
Of dancing wavelets
Tiptoeing ballet
To a rising sun.
Then why come
Charging
On foam-flecked horses
Prancing and rearing
To spoil our fun?
No bits nor bridles
Between teeth wearing
But broken spars
In your fury breaking.

Then lo!
All is peaceful and calm again.

HEART ATTACK AND THE
DRUNKEN BALLET DANCERS

Almost thirty years ago came another milestone in my life. I was still working hard, this time preparing a chimney breast to take a much larger fireplace, a job that entailed cutting away some very hard concrete with steel chisels. My arms ached but I didn't want to admit that I felt tired, until the Easter Sunday morning that I tried to stop a stubborn cow getting onto the roadway as the Circuit of Ireland Motor Rally was passing by. Then it struck: a sudden pain in both wrists, a bursting, breathtaking pain in the centre of my chest. If only I could pass some gas up or down, what a relief it would give. But no, a giant vice-grip held my heart, refusing to let go. I knew enough about life that I never took death seriously. I also knew that panic was not the best medicine for a heart attack. This brings to mind a fisherman skipper, who observed from his wheelhouse that his crew seemed excited about fishing gear that was badly entangled on deck. He emerged from the wheelhouse and said in a loud voice: 'Now men, if there is to be panic, let it be orderly.' When Dr O'Shea arrived, he gave me an injection and asked me how I felt, saying: 'You know, Mike, you could die!' I told him in rather blasphemous terms what I thought of the Grim Reaper.

The fifty-mile journey to Tralee Hospital was the 'slow boat to hell'. Strapped to a steel ladder-like stretcher, I felt every pothole, bump and hollow. It seemed more like being strapped to the back of a farmer's harrow when sewing spring oats. I conked out on two occasions. The ambulance pulled into the roadside and I was given oxygen. My daughter Anne and a nurse were with me. Anne whispered: 'We are entering the hospital grounds, Dad. You are a very patient man, you never complained or panicked.' I was too ill to tell her I had used orderly panic. The hospital doctor gave me a further injection. I was attached to a monitor and made comfortable. The pain was abating and 'peace came dropping slow'. Anne said: 'Goodnight, Dad. I'll see you tomorrow.' To quote Coleridge's Ancient Mariner:

> To Mary Queen the praise be given!
> She sent the gentle sleep from Heaven,
> That slid unto my soul.

Several times during the night, the watchful eye of the 'lady in white' lingered close to the pallet of the stricken hero, listening to my breathing and glancing at the wavy lines of my heartbeat on the screen of the monitor.

'Are you feeling all right?'

'Yes, thank you, nurse!'

Another day dawned. I felt weak but comfortable and they put a needle in my arm, tubed to a bottle. This, I was told, was the drip. My wife Peggy and my family visited me often. I now began to realize how fortunate I was to be alive. A farmer in middle age was brought in, but only lasted a few hours. A travelling man was recovering but refused to give a blood sample because of some old custom in his clan.

After several days in the intensive-care ward, I was transferred to the general ward. I wondered at first if I had been moved to some mental institution. I was astonished to see, in the dim night light of the ward, two pyjama-clad figures waltzing on a highly polished floor, to the accompaniment of their singing – 'Daisy, Daisy, give me your answer, do!' I was not prepared for entertainment such as this. I sat bolt upright in my bed. The man in the neighbouring bed leaned over and said: 'That's the French sailor and Jimmy Kelly. They found a bottle of whiskey somewhere. They waited until the lights were dimmed to drink it. They are harmless young lads. The sailor is being treated for pneumonia. Kelly is to be treated for his back.' By the look of him, there was nothing wrong with his back. The waltzing became more hilarious when the Frenchman started a ballet-like South American dance. The man next to me, whom I got to know later as Johnny, exclaimed: 'I own to Christ, if someone happens to fall, he'll break his bloody arse!' At that moment a night nurse entered the ward and tried to get the dancers back to bed. The sailor was quick to obey, but Jimmy kept insisting that the nurse dance with him. She went across the room and spoke briefly on the phone. Two men in white coats entered the ward and asked Jimmy to behave and go back to bed. By this time Jimmy was losing his cool, only to find himself swiftly held prone on the bed like a trussed fowl while an injection was administered. In a few short minutes Jimmy seemed to get very drowsy. Between yawns he kept singing little snatches of: 'The songs that were sung' ... yawn ... 'the days when we were young' ... yawn! Jimmy's head hit the pillow. The nurse wheeled up a cot with a high railing. Jimmy was placed carefully inside and made comfortable. The rails were closed, leaving Waltzing Matilda to sleep it off. Not a peep was heard from the French sailor.

The day nurses arrived early, as dawn was breaking. They had some difficulty in waking Johnny. 'Wake up,

John! It's six o'clock. We must make your bed.' John opened his eyes and gave a prolonged yawn: 'Excuse me, nurse, it was one long whore of a night.' The good nurse didn't seem to hear. I was being educated and entertained. An old bachelor farmer's bed was lined up near that of the sailor's. They never seemed to hit it off. The Frenchman would say: 'If you give me your address, I can get you a nice French wife.'

The farmer would retort: 'I don't want your French wife, or any wife for that matter.'

'Oh! French girl keep you warm. Maybe she kiss you! She make love all night! Do you hear?'

'I hear you! Shut up! You're only fit for telling lies.'

Some of the exchanges were special gems of craic and banter. The matron carried out an inspection of all the lockers because of the drunken ballet dancers. The empty Paddy bottle was found standing by the wall, but dead men tell no tales.

Jimmy would come over and sit on the end of my bed. The sailor also became a very good friend. We had a lot in common to talk about. A friend from Dublin brought me a bottle of whiskey, which I shared with the sailor and Kelly. This time we divided the beverage into Lucozade bottles and hid the empty bottle in the rubbish bin. One nurse said the ward smelled like a brewery.

Day by day I felt stronger, until eventually I was discharged. I was told I had angina and that I would have to live with it. I was to walk two and a half miles per day. I was to take two Trasicor, one Aldactide, one Centyl K and three Lanoxin a day. I had damaged my heart, but the heart is a wonder, sometimes building itself up again. If I was careful I might live three years or more – a consoling thought! I was also advised to get my things in order: paperwork etc. Having at least three years to get my paperwork done, the first job I did was to paper the front room, just in case I might snuff it!

I was called to my first check-up in Tralee. A young Indian doctor checked my heart and blood pressure. He assured me that I didn't have angina. I was to take more exercise and walk five miles a day. From that day onwards I decided I would change my lifestyle. First things first: I stopped smoking for good, gave up mutton, ate very little butter or sugar. I also tried to be careful about salt. A beef stew once a week using no frying pan and very little bacon, plenty of white cabbage, boiled onions, oatmeal gruel, carrots and parsnips. I never spilled the water of any vegetable down the sink: I drank all the juices. I ate mackerel in any form, fresh and smoked; white fish and salmon; chicken, skinned and roasted; raw celery; garlic; parsley and turnips; whole grapefruit; no junk foods or biscuits; only home-made bread.

I can make fish soups from any kind of shellfish: limpets, crab, razor and all types of clams, mussels and lobsters. I love the common wrasse and skinned gurnard. Even several kinds of edible seaweed can be added to soup, with segments of sea urchin. Crab claws give edge to the appetite, but do not allay hunger. Fish roe of herring, cod and whiting are full of minerals as are, in fact, the roe of all fish. A mackerel in season should cook in its own oil. Too much mineral oil and cooking fat are to be avoided. Fish oil will never create wax or clog the arteries. I drink the water in which salmon is boiled, mixed with a little onion and garlic, with a touch of black pepper and salt. It is very savoury. Only very lean beef should be consumed. I cut out all fudge, cream, cakes and fizzy drinks. I like an occasional drink of whiskey, never brandy. Citrus fruits, grapes, pears, plums and apples must never be taken in excess: they may trigger severe acid indigestion. Along with natural sugar and vitamins, fruit also contains a high degree of acid. Christmas plum pudding, chocolate, whipped cream, tinned fruits and fancy buns only remind me of splitting headaches – they are not for people with wonky hearts!

When I told my doctor of the things I had eliminated from my diet he said: 'You're surely for the birds, Mike! If you cut out any more, you'll starve to death!'

Walking against the hill must be practised with patience, in order to put a little workload on the heart. Deep breathing of pure fresh air, a good sleep and a good hearty laugh can help you cheat the impending heart attack and the Grim Reaper himself.

The Mountain Road

Each morning I walk the mountain road,
Yet some ask why I try to climb,
What do I hope to find up there
Where small birds put song into mine ear,
Telling me that God is near.
And maybe you can tell Him
That you care, that you are sorry,
Or better still, that you love Him.
The mountain road is perfumed
With spring's reborn flowers
And God will teach me
To forget this human dream
And bid me walk with Him awhile
In His immortal spring,
Within the mountain road.

MY GARDEN

The kiss of the sun for pardon,
The song of the birds for mirth,
One is nearer God's Heart in a garden
Than anywhere else on earth.

I have forgotten who composed this poem [Dorothy
Frances Gurney – ed.] or where I first heard the words
but it became indelibly stored in some cell of my brain.
It surfaced immediately when my mind or inner-some-
thing triggered the idea: Why not write an essay describing a country garden? Then suddenly up popped the
poem that I use here as an introduction. Perhaps an emi-
nent brain surgeon will produce some breakthrough
data on the grey matter.

Now, in the evening of my days, and especially when
road-walking has become so hazardous, the confines of
my garden are more than a safe haven. I regard it as a
peaceful, God-given sanctuary, a place where I have time
to rest, to reflect and to observe the little things that I
didn't even have a thought fo; the trivial natural happenings that I was too busy to observe, being too concerned earning the crust of that daily bread. For that
matter, isn't our entire island a garden? The Garden of
Eden? Please, do not bring that one up – I do not want
any serpents. I do not want to get evicted by some belted
earl landlord of the British Empire, the Irish Republic,

the EEC or any other global, dominating empires that say they want peace in the garden. Yes! I have bushes in my garden, but my garden is a Kerry garden.

I have discovered some very important things in my garden, most of all peace of mind; time to listen to faint little twitterings, different notes and sudden flutterings near at hand. I discovered that I also had inquisitive company when a red robin came bobbing along one day. I fed it with breadcrumbs and other titbits of fat. Then it introduced its little fledgling to join in this unorthodox hospitality, call it what you will, Simon Community or meals on wheels. Well, it worked. The offspring thrived. The breast feathers soon became pink, losing the drab colour of a fledgling. Then a blackbird discovered what was happening in the garden. No doubt some loose bird-talk spread the news! Magpies, jackdaws and crows converged on the scene and would stand daringly, letting off steam in a scolding, chattering chorus of criticism and indignation, or perhaps pleading to be fed. However, my diplomatic department has failed to crack the code of bird-talk and for that alone I am thankful. If Big Brother ever gets that far, all wild birds will have to stick their beaks in the sand.

Now, the blackbird with the yellow bill was clever. He introduced his wife to the freeloading. By the way, his wife's name in Gaelic is *céirseach*. She is not too much concerned with music and wears very drab clothes, not the shiny velvet black of her musical husband, *londubh*. I have no doubt she is a most diligent, hard-working housewife, always feeding and taking care of the children; a real homemaker. I cannot understand how she married him in the first place, who made the match, where she came from or whether Mr Londubh was cast into a deep sleep and a rib taken from his side. If so, he is stuck with her for good. I will not ask Darwin or Einstein. Perhaps their answer is outdated. I remember a little rhyme from my schoolbook:

> Birdie with the yellow bill,
> Hopped upon my window sill
> Cocked his shining eye and said,
> 'Ain't you shamed, you sleepy head?'
>   (Robert Louis Stevenson)

Now, perhaps I am guilty of rash judgment. If so, I crave forgiveness. I have heard from sources of authority that the male blackbird assists in the construction of the nest, the feeding of both wife and chicks, taking a turn to sit on the eggs to keep them at their proper temperature. If *céirseach* needs exercise or food during the hatching period, the male will sing not directly over the nest but at a distance, which misleads predators seeking to find its exact location. If a predator comes too near, the bird will utter a loud, chattering alarm cry and will attack if possible.

In my garden was a pair of wrens of our smallest species, the gold-crested wren. They were very elusive. Our brown wren, *dreoilín* in Gaelic, can burst into sweet, short bouts of song. The magpie is a murderous, ferocious pirate who will hunt, destroy and consume young chicks and eggs. Other enemies are stoats, greyback crows and cats. I do my best to protect my songsters. Last summer, after having read some humbug treatise dealing with reincarnation, while sitting in my garden seat, there was my robin staring me in the face. I concluded that it was time to issue a warning. Addressing the bird, I said: 'If you are my good mother Mary Cremin, RIP, you better get the hell out of here or you could wind up in the belly of the cat!' However, it didn't seem to work with my robin.

Not alone is bird life interesting, one must also consider insects. The honeybee seems to be attracted to a special dahlia. The bees in question are light brown in colour. I watched as they seemed to work in unending relays, tanking up and flying away. I noticed they always flew in a southerly direction, while others kept coming in from the same direction. This sequence continued until late evening. They certainly work late and early, gathering honey for the hive. I also noticed some bees crawling near the plant as if they were half-asleep and after a period of time they would come to life and fly off. This was explained to me by a professional beekeeper. He said they were young bees that suffered from consuming too much nectar. They become intoxicated and suffer from a slight hangover, from which they have to rest for a while until they recover and fly back to the hive. I did not invent this; I have to believe the authority that explains it.

I have tried to meditate by closing my eyes and ears to all worldly anxiety, attempting to release myself from the material woe of the existing universe, transcending to a higher plane, praying and repeating a mantra. I usually drop off to sleep. It seemed to me that I was peering down into a vast tunnel of dark, peaceful emptiness. Maybe if I continue in my search for the light I will find it. Presently I will trust and say, like Newman: 'Lead kindly light, the night is dark and I am far from home.'

Having awakened from my fanciful garden dream, I noticed a flying insect cut circular pieces from the green leaves of rose bushes and fly off. Imagine a wasp-like fly, using a sharp saw or serrated tool, cutting out a piece of leaf to be used, I have been informed, as a lining for its nest. It is very fastidious about which leaves it carves. Dangerous area, my garden! I could have my leg amputated!

Of course my garden is a very private, peaceful place, or at least it is meant to be. I admit that this is not always the case. Only yesterday I had to intervene in a real free-for-all between what I assume were two cock robins engaged in mortal combat. On my intervention they grudgingly flew off with some rumpled feathers and bloody beaks. Were they fighting for territory, or was there some dispute concerning marital relations or maybe girlfriends? It is sad to think that the urge to kill is the ultimate solution.

Soft April showers and bright mayflowers will bring the summer back again, also the aphids, and many species of blackfly and greenfly that produce spores and fungus, bringing disease and decay to many beautiful flowers and shrubs. The gardener must also deal with several different species of snails and slugs, with acid rain and salt spray thrown in. All is not rosy in the garden or in wild nature. We hear about the balance of nature. Was there ever a perfect balance or is it a perpetual fight for survival? I do not know the answer; I am only asking myself.

I sincerely believe that each individual is entitled to a period of undisturbed sleep, be it by night or day. Now, one night when a serene tranquility enveloped my garden and I was fast asleep, I was rudely awakened by a wild, piercing shriek. I found that I was disturbed by the caterwauling of the feline species. Why do they make such an outcry? Some define this as 'catting', others say it is the ineffable rapture of lovemaking. Feline sex suggests to me a rapacious form of procreation.

Why all the rampaging, rip-roaring rumpus, culminating in a wild, unearthly shriek causing every canine in the neighbourhood to bark and howl?

Nature has many strange, mysterious ways of dealing with the procreation of the species. I do not want to create a border between male and female cats but I honestly think that a case could be made for compromise on both sides: females on neutral ground and toms bound to a curfew and ceasefire. If this could be implemented, poor unfortunate Humpty-Dumpty might enjoy a good sleep and not become a somnambulist.

One is never really sure what to expect in a garden. Only last year I was regaled by a nocturnal visitor in the form of a screech owl. Fortunately, it was before bedtime. I directed a flashlight on the branch where it perched cat-faced, looking down at me. When I attempted to mimic the wise visitor, it was more than it could take and, giving me a departing half-hoot, half-screech, it flapped its great wings, disappearing into the night.

> A wise old owl
> Stood on an oak,
> The more it heard
> The less it spoke.
> The less it spoke
> The more it heard.
> Let's imitate this wise old bird.
> (Edward Hersey Richards)

At the start of this essay I described my garden as a God-given sanctuary, a place where I could rest, find peace and time to reflect. Now, on second thoughts or perhaps awakening from my reverie, I must accuse myself of floundering in a morass of sheer hypocrisy. I think I have read somewhere in the Bible: 'What hast thou got that was not given unto thee?' I do not realize my errors, finding myself in direct conflict with nature itself, thinking myself secure within my greedy, begrudging self-made enclave, lording it over the fowl and the brute. I only wanted special birds, special animals, special flowers, roses and shrubs, special everything in my garden. I had no time for love-cats, owls, jackdaws, magpies and ravens. I could not tolerate nature's wild whims disturbing my sleep, never even giving a thought to the fact that I had entombed myself within a fortress of self-gratification, when suddenly I was confronted with a startling truth: 'Behold the lilies of the field, they neither reap nor spin. Yet Solomon in all his glory was not clothed as one of these.' (Matt. 6: 28)

Now descending from my thinly gilded throne, admitting my faults with humility, I arrive full circle back at the beginning of my composition: 'One is nearer God's heart in a garden / Than anywhere else on earth.'

Ode to a Wren

Many little mouths
To feed!
How do they cradle
Them all
In mossy green
House
With feather-lined
Wall?

Busy brown mothers
With laugh
And with shout,
Nervous little fathers
Keep bobbing about.

No doctor's bottles,
No fuss and no frills,
No contraceptives,
No fertility pills.

A PAINTING IS BORN

To me all nature – sea, land, clouds, mountains, valleys, rocks, flowering plants and grasses – is an enigma. I feel that I too am part of nature's picture.

Maybe the awesome immensity of the plan becomes too weighty for my curious, mundane intrusion. Then why do I not close the window of my niggling curiosity to be enveloped again in the darkness of my coming, lest the light that has illuminated my birth becomes the torment of my going? At present, I stay with the Psalmist, saying: 'O Lord, I love the beauty of thy house and the place where thy glory dwelleth.' Now, having wrestled with myself, words and mind trying to outwit my inquisitive investigation, I find myself bogged down on beholding the bountiful things that surround me in their natural beauty.

What part do I play in this plan? Am I, like Shakespeare's Hamlet, only 'a poor player that struts and frets his hour upon the stage'? Does my life culminate in dusty death, as he suggests? Please, Willie, let poor Yorick escape at least from the gloom of a paradise lost! I do not want the jackpot, only some of the peace and tranquility that is here for the taking.

I assume that no two humans have the same minds. During the time I earned my living fishing in the company of other fishermen, hundreds and thousands of mackerel passed by and through our hands. We often tried to find a pair of mackerel with the exact same skin patterns, but failed. Scientists tell us that no two snow crystals are the same. Does this prove that we are part and parcel of nature's specially graded species? I think it is only fair, if we are all somewhat different, that we should refrain from sermonizing to each other from our divergent points of view.

Snow crystals become the silken, shimmering, glittering raiment of the mighty peaks of mountains. Man's false ego may tempt him to disturb the beauty of a glacier filled with snow crystals. Too often he becomes engulfed in an avalanche of nature's beauty or perhaps of his own vain ego. Beauty in the eye of the beholder may become a Hydra-headed monster, creating greed and desire. I only ponder, wonder and wait for a little chink in the armour of this beautiful, unending yet terrifying, infinite cosmos. I can only hope to learn that I, puny man, am part of the enigma of nature.

Now, why did I attempt to paint a picture in the first place? Truly it came from within. Maybe a pregnancy of the mind, wanting to emulate with the crudest strokes of a brush the mountains and landscape that surround me daily. The phenomenal, ever-changing kaleidoscope of light and shade when clouds momentarily obscure the sun, instantly changing the colour of the landscape into a sequence of different hues, adds to the difficulty of the artist who aspires to imitate.

On a summer's day can be seen the serenity and bloom of meadows and mountains in a distant dreamy, hazy, bluish shade of purple; clouds of cumuli in perfect complementary colour, all blending harmoniously into the ethereal arch of infinity. Surely the scene is composed by the divine will of some god-artist, painter of nature and of our very being. On the other side of the canvas we see the awesome power, yet terrifying grandeur, of a violent storm, in which little waves become mountainous crashing seas, venting, washing, spilling and spending a spume-blown, foaming fury on shingle beaches and rock-bound headlands. A good ship can be seen wallowing between breaking billows, her patient master anxiously guiding, tending, shepherding, and finally bringing her back from the brink of impending doom.

On reaching my seventieth birthday I finally decided to satisfy the consuming, pent-up desire to paint the beautiful scene that had confronted me since my childhood. If memory serves me right I pondered, mulled and minded what kind of materials I would need. Having decided, I murmured to my wife Peggy: 'Here goes nothing.' Clomping out of the back door, I caught the end of her retort: 'At this hour of your life, it's your prayers you should be thinking of!'

In a shed at the back of the house I kept all kinds of bric-a-brac. Faithfully awaiting me on a shelf I found some small tubes of oils that I had bought some time previously, and also several rusted tins of paint, some of which had only a few inches of thickened paint in the bottom. I suddenly imagined the ghost of Little Boy Blue standing in the attic surveying his toys, some covered with dust and rust, and the beautiful ending of the poem depicting his childhood innocence: 'Ay, faithful to Little Boy Blue they stand, / Since he kissed them and put them there.' Alas, I fit, not into the category of childhood innocence, but the category of 'gone with the wind'! I found a saw and a piece of hardboard that my son was using. He obligingly cut me a rectangular piece, twenty inches by eighteen inches. I told him I was to become the new Picasso. He didn't seem surprised, just said: 'Why not!'

My paints, as I remember, were a motley mix of colours. I used raw linseed oil and some turpentine and a drying agent called terpene. After a long period of stirring, pouring, thinning, mixing and experimenting, at last I painted a sky of hazy, light blue-green. Not a cloud in view; I called it eggshell blue, but for the life of me I could never tell what species of bird laid that colour egg. I waited several days for my cloudless sky to dry out. Probably it suffered a hangover from my generosity with raw linseed, plus my trial and error.

Next morning I gazed longingly at the mountains beyond Ballinskelligs Bay that I knew so well: Hog's Head and the curving hills stretching eastward and upward; to the south the majestic mountains of Beara nodding their heads with chieftain-bearing pride in the background; Deenish Island and Scarrif Island westward, sheltering the entrance to the bay. I employed some makeshift tools of my own, such as a half-inch black bristle brush used for painting windows and an old steel writing pen with a wooden handle that I found effective for drawing lines. Pieces of rag and scraps of foam came into play and as I progressed I even tried using the tip of my right forefinger. This tended to lead to a somewhat messy kind of art, and so I was obliged to demote the promoted finger back to its original index position.

I painted the near hills with every colour I thought possible. To match the scene I painted in some little blotches like clouds of grey and white, and a very calm serene sea with glossy reflections. All in all, I felt pleased with my first effort. I did not receive any great recognition or encouragement from anybody, except friendly remarks such as: 'I suppose it's nice!', 'Well, I wouldn't know really!' and 'Are they pictures of cows in the sky?'

This was the last straw, enough to make poor Picasso take a flying jump into the bay. Months passed. My masterpiece stood nakedly without frame, fame or recognition in a dim corner near the fireplace. My enthusiasm for future creativity in the world of painting seemed to suffer a deflective downward curve. Despite that, a fervour and an ardent flame still burned within my mind.

I confess to feeling pangs of regret on the day that Peggy and I decided that the picture had served its purpose and it was now to be consigned to its original birthplace in the shed behind the house, and to the limbo of my unfulfilled dream. On my way out to dispose of the painting, Peggy said: 'Wait a moment, I see somebody at the front door.' I laid the painting on the kitchen table, face upwards, before opening the door. Two men stood there, and upon inviting them inside, they told me that they were interested in information regarding Skelligs Rock and the possibility of a boat trip there. After exchanging some pleasantries and graciously thanking me, much to my surprise one of the men approached the kitchen table and, taking the picture in his hands, he asked: 'Who painted this?'

He introduced himself as a person who held a distinction from an academy of art, and accompanying him was a student from that school. I humbly asked for his evaluation of the work. His reply was as follows: 'If I was asked to give an evaluation, I would have to give it full marks for colour, blending and distribution, including natural perspective of mountains.' He then asked if anyone had given me tuition, to which question I truthfully answered in the negative. The good man advised me to study nature as it appeared to me and not depend on books. His words and generous appreciation helped to free my mind. Immediately I became part of the sea, wind and shadow of the hillside. I felt free. I could sing again:

> Oh! Had I the wings of a dove
> To soar through the blue sunny sky
> By what breeze would my pinions be stirred?
> To what beautiful land would I fly?
> Though the gorgeous east allures
> And the light of the southern skies
> Fain would I roam from my island home
> For skies more fair.

Thus ends the narrative of my initial experimental involvement with oil painting, from which I have received so much joy and intense pleasure, seeking to emulate the beauty of nature, the elusive mystery of the now and hereafter. That first painting is one of my most treasured possessions, now hanging in pride of place over the fireplace in my living room.

Who Scattered the Stars?

Hark! From the abyss
Of darkness
A mighty rumbling roared,
Likened
To a voice-command:
'Roll back, dark night!
My blinding stars
Will fill
The infinite
With light.
I do not toll
A funeral bell
For you!
I give you life,
I fill the seas,
And rock is born,
Where angry wind
Lays battle to a wave.'

Dewdrops glisten
Like diamond glass.
Moonbeams spin
Silk spiders' skeins
Of fairy silk
Among morning stalks
Of grass.

It is time to scatter the stars,
Time to light a thousand

Billion lamps,
To pebble-dash a beach,
Wood a forest,
And flow a river.
Time to banish serpents,
Time to seek the spirit,
Time to be crucified
With love.
Time to wonder,
Time to ponder,
Time to stand in awe,
Trying to understand
Who scattered the stars.

A GARDEN: IN THE WANING
LIGHT OF MY YEARS

Time was when I walked the highways and byways, the hills and valleys of my native townland without let or hindrance, carefree, young and healthy. I did not notice the flowers, the trees, birds or bees, even myself. I never gave a thought to who I was, except that I strutted by on two legs. All other animated creatures shunned my presence. In a lighter vein I could be likened to Topsy in *Uncle Tom's Cabin*, who, when asked where she came from, retorted: 'I 'specs I growed.' A friend of mine in Nova Scotia, when asked where she came from, said: 'I think we were here always.'

The fact of the matter is that I am now old and frail. I glimpse the Grim Reaper stalking his prey. I await the inevitable: 'Sceptre and Crown must tumble down, / And in the dust be equal made.' (James Shirley)

In front of my cottage by the roadside is a postage-stamp lawn, sheltered on both sides by privet and hawthorn hedges, with a couple of fir trees here and there. The only furniture is an old wooden garden seat where I rest and often droop into the sleep of the ending, as foretold in Gaelic folklore:

Deireadh fir a shuan
Agus an bhean á faire féin suas.

The man sleeping his last
And the woman alert in the sleep of the ending.

The old road is now a modern two-lane highway with no space for pedestrians, especially those who have three legs at eventide. Once again the old Gaelic riddle comes to mind:

> *Ceithre cosa ar maidin*
> *Dhá chos i lár an lae*
> *Agus trí chosa um thráthnona.*

The folklorist condenses the lifespan of an aged person into one day:

> On all fours as a child in the morning of life,
> Two legs at midday
> Three legs at eventide, an old person walking with
> the aid of a stick.

Now in the waning light of my years on this planet named Earth, I prepare for the natural departure that awaits all life, including the most dominant and exceedingly clever human being called by anthropologists and scientists Homo sapiens, Homo erectus, etc. I respect and try to understand the wisdom of these great scholars as best I can, sure of one reality: that I too will disappear into the mist of timelessness. My piece of animated clay will return into the earth from where it was formed, hoping that the spirit will return to its creator. Life seems so vainglorious, the answers still 'blowing in the wind'. Nevertheless, it brings to mind many fanciful echoes of youth and memories of the past.

Now confined to my garden seat, I put up the shutters and close my eyes, repeat a mantra and try to find God somewhere out there in the unending, perpetual tunnel of darkness of my own doubting mind. In this unresponsive, lethargic mood, Morpheus, the Roman god of sleep, must have intervened. I awakened, startled by a dream, to find it was already twilight. I regard dreams as foolish fantasies of the mind, but not this one. Deep within the darkening shadows of failing light I could imagine a lone, kneeling figure with upraised hands, imploring and crying out to His Father for help to ease His physical suffering. Could I not watch one hour with Him? I had slept peacefully through it all, abandoning Him in his anguish. Was this the garden that triggered memories of far-flung days of my youth? Father Colm O'Riordan and Father Andrew Collins, two Jesuit priests, often visited and sat with me outside my roadside cottage while on holidays in Ballinskelligs. One worked the mission fields of Rhodesia. The other gave his all in a dreadful leper colony. Farewell, you warriors of Christ! Enjoy your paradise. Nobody said it was going to be easy.

My Lovely Skellig's Shore

This night my heart is heavy,
My eyes are dim with tears.
In memory I'm taken back
To boyhood days of yore,
Where I lived in happy childhood
By my lovely Skellig's shore.

There, in springtime of the year
The young bright flowers, they show.
The lily and the violet blue
And golden primrose blow.
Dakota's hills are beautiful,
The Texan plains and more –
I'd leave them all to walk again
My lovely Skellig's shore.

Kinnard and Coom stand side by side
Where the road comes winding down.
In the valley stands supreme and grand
Old Canuig Mountain brown.
The huntsman's pack has waked the morn,
I hear the hillside roar.
Ah, rue the day I went away
From my lovely Skellig's shore!

Kilreelig fair beyond compare,
Its shady dales and dells
Where golden furze and woodbine mix
With purple heather bells.

Oft-times I joined the seine boatmen
And pulled the long clamp oar,
When we hunted shoals of mackerel
By my lovely Skellig's shore.

A mist comes on the islands
And the mountains of my heart.
Your castle and the shining sands
Are tearing me apart.
The crossroad dance
Where lovers glance,
I ne'er will see you more,
The melodeon softly tuning
By my lovely Skellig's shore.

A sadness clouds my heart tonight,
When I know I cannot go
To lay my bones in Ireland
But on a foreign shore.
No neighbours kind will wake me,
No funeral sad and slow
To lay me down in Abbey ground,
By my lovely Skellig's shore.

Farewell to Ballinskelligs!
I may never see you more,
The castle and the Abbey
That stand beside the shore.
Your purple hills so beautiful,
I'll miss you ever more,
Farewell to Ballinskelligs
And my lovely Skellig's shore.

AFTERWORD

As Michael Kirby's English-language publisher, I shall add my meed of reminiscence to earlier tributes.

A man of fantastical imagination and a radiant smile, this kindly, aboriginally sculpted Viking bestrode the century past. (He loved these pseudo-racial categories, playing with them in a mix of scorn and bemusement that befitted the twinkle in his imperious hazel eyes.)

In May 1991 he came to a Lilliput Press launch in Dunsany Castle on the occasion of the paperback publication of *Seventy Years Young* by Daisy Fingall. There he met another Irishman, a warrior of a different stripe, Randal, Lord Dunsany, and the two old boys talked at length, comparing the rich, deep clays of eastern Meath with the thinner soils of the south Iveragh, and remembering their ancestors, the one native, the other Norman. He also met my mother, a Wilson of Presbyterian origins from Ulster, another 'settler' family, and she spoke of ploughing with six in hand when diesel was scarce during the 1930s – clearly someone to reckon with, he felt admiringly.

His intense solicitude and interest in family transferred to my own children and womenfolk as we took our holidays at Kinnard where his mother's people came from, a few hundred yards above his own dwelling in Ballinskelligs. He had restored and re-roofed the small farmhouse with his sons on behalf of its German owner, a dentist who'd purchased it in the 1970s.

Michael suffered my monoglot ways with supreme courtesy, and we rarely talked politics. I sensed though a deep undertow of hurt, an unhealed wound inflicted during the War of Independence and Civil War of 1919-23, which had set brother against brother in this most partisan of counties. He enjoyed meeting his peers and on one memorable evening in early 1999 on St Brigid's Day, at the onset of the Celtic spring, I brought a fellow Kerryman and Lilliput author, the poet-philosopher John Moriarty, to his house to meet him. To witness these two great spirits rejoicing in each other and in communion was a privilege.

The physicality and actuality of time and place were all in all to Michael. As we walked the boreens those late summers, picking early blackberries, we debated texts, gossiped mildly and interrogated the landscape with its fresh crop of holiday 'homes' that added skeletal layers to the Bronze Age settlements strewn across the higher slopes of the valley.

His own layered beliefs were profoundly pre-Christian and animist. He gladly wore the cloak of a formal, inherited faith, which he would shrug aside from time to time, displaying its scarlet lining, and his pagan, beating heart beneath. While the world that Michael describes in his writings is pre-industrial, he lived to encounter cyberspace with an all-encompassing curiosity.

Here was a true celebrant: tender, capable of ferocity, while wondrously innocent in the face of the universe. His books are his memorials.